HOW WE DRAFTED

ADLAI

STEVENSON

L. C. catalog card number: 55-6073

© Walter Johnson, 1955

THIS IS A BORZOI BOOK,
PUBLISHED BY ALFRED A. KNOPF, INC.

FIRST EDITION

HOW WE DRAFTED
ADLAI
STEVENSON

Walter Johnson

NEW YORK · ALFRED A. KNOPF
1955

TO

SENATOR J. W. FULBRIGHT OF ARKANSAS

STATESMAN

OF

VISION, INTEGRITY, AND COURAGE

FOREWORD

THE NOMINATION of Adlai Stevenson for President on the Democratic Party ticket in 1952 was unique. Although nominees had been drafted before—Charles Evans Hughes in 1916 and James Garfield in 1880—this was the first draft in which citizens without assignment played a major role.

The role was not unique only because of the results achieved, but also because these citizens helped organize the machinery of the draft. Whether Adlai Stevenson would have been nominated if there had been no Draft Stevenson Committee is not for members of that committee to say.

This book was written to record what occurred, as it occurred, and why—in so far as we had direct knowledge of it and participated in it.

If there is any question about the use of direct quotations from people in those hectic days of the Convention, this is the place perhaps to point out that I kept detailed notes of the conversations and of the meetings recorded in this book.

The Convention story is related here on a day-by-day—and frequently hour-by-hour—basis as the only means of revealing the tempo, the tension, and the impact of events and explaining in proper perspective the major aspects of our work. On occasion we had to find a phrase that would explain what we were doing. This frequently was given to us in various forms by some members of the press, radio, and TV corps; they said we were using a new language in political responsibility.

In fairness to the truth, if we were using a new language in politics, it was that we were conscientiously reflecting what Adlai E. Stevenson had infused into the American scene.

The experience we as citizens had at the Democratic National Convention is heartening. It shows that citizens do not necessarily need money in politics if they have conviction and integrity of purpose in a cause that has high merits of its own and if they have the willingness to participate in making political decisions.

CONTENTS

CHAPTER

I   *Stevenson: the Man*   3

II   *Launching the Stevenson Draft: February to July 14*   18

III   *Opening Convention Headquarters: Monday, Tuesday, Wednesday, July 14, 15, 16*   42

IV   *Stimulating Interest in the Draft: Wednesday, Thursday, Friday, July 16, 17, 18*   60

V   *The Delegates Come to See Us: Wednesday, Thursday, Friday, July 16, 17, 18*   74

VI   *Pennsylvania Holds the Key: Saturday, July 19*   85

VII   *The Draft Finds a Floor Leader: Sunday, July 20*   98

VIII   *The Opening Day of the Convention: Monday, July 21*   104

IX   *The Stevenson Bandwagon Rolls: Tuesday, July 22*   115

X   *Placing Stevenson's Name in Nomination: Wednesday, Thursday, July 23–4*   134

XI *The Draft Cannot be Stopped: Thursday,
     Friday, July 24–5*   144

XII *Who Drafted Adlai Stevenson?*   156

ACKNOWLEDGMENTS   171

INDEX   *follows page* 172

HOW WE DRAFTED

ADLAI

STEVENSON

CHAPTER I

STEVENSON: THE MAN

EVERY SEAT in the National Guard Armory in Washington was taken on that Saturday evening of March 29, 1952. There was a hint of spring in the air, and politicians' thoughts were turning ever more steadily toward politics. For this was no ordinary year, but a Presidential election year, the time of the high harvest.

Inside the Armory the band played over and over the theme song of the assembled faithful: "Happy Days Are Here Again." Man after man spoke, each seen and also heard. The hall overflowed with "greatness," for, by that amiable convention of our partisan political gatherings, every speaker was described by the chairman as a "great Democrat and a great American."

Meanwhile the fifty-three hundred diners—at one hundred dollars a plate—pursuing the curious ritual by which we eat ourselves into good works or political salvation, made their way through fruit cocktail, filet mignon, ice cream, and coffee. Sated now, but curious, they pushed back their chairs to hear the evening's principal speaker.

Would he? Or wouldn't he? For months the answer to these queries had been vainly sought by press and politicians. The small man who held the answer to the questions hugged it to his breast; indeed, he seemed to take a boyish delight in withholding the secret he cherished.

Suddenly the crowd heard the words of that unadorned, most dignified of introductions: "The President of the United States."

Then they heard the man who looked as so many of his fellows look; the homey man with the Midwestern voice; the man, lonely in his isolation even from his own party, who almost single-handedly had won election to the Presidency when "experts" gave him little chance of winning.

It was the old-fashioned, ripsnorting, "give-'em-hell" speech that President Truman had made so often, and often so successfully. It pictured the Democrats as progressive and the Republicans as reactionary, as "dinosaurs"; the one party the nation's savior, the other its potential destroyer. The speaker's gestures irregularly stressed the beat of the spoken words, and, his denunciations of Republicans growing warmer, members of the crowd yelled: "Pour it on 'em!"

The speaker, obviously enjoying himself, gave no hint of things to come. He was merely, it appeared, making another partisan talk to the faithful. But suddenly, with no change of stress or pace, they heard these words interpolated into the prepared speech:

I shall not be a candidate for re-election. I have served my country long and I think efficiently and honestly. I shall not accept a renomination. I do not feel it is my duty to spend another four years in the White House.

The stunned audience was silent for a moment. Then there arose loud groans of "No, no!" from all over the hall. They proceeded from the shocked disbelief of some. They fell from the lips of men who saw themselves losing their jobs; from other men who had a deep affection for the leader who had announced his coming retirement from public life. But now the gnawing question had been definitively answered. Harry S. Truman would not seek the Democratic nomination for the Presidency in 1952.

Yet immediately this question had been answered —indeed, because it had been answered—there arose other questions. Who would be the candidates for the nomination? Who was highest in the qualities of "availability"? Who would have the opportunity of competing for the grand prize: election to the most powerful secular office in the world?

Were those likely to seek the nomination of the stature needed to match the seriousness of the times? Did they have the experience, the intellectual training, and the dedication to reason that this age of turmoil demanded? With a twenty-year record of having led the country out of the depths of a grim depression, through the turbulent years of war and the recurring crises of the postwar years, could the party find a man endowed with the qualities required to lead the nation forward in the new era?

These questions were posed on that night of March 29 in Washington. They would not be answered until another night in Chicago in July.

If the crowd, bewildered by what it had just heard, stood uncertainly in the Armory, the reporters present knew what they wanted. With a deep sense of the needs of the time, they made a beeline for a man who stood talking to a little knot of people at the head table. He was a medium-sized, balding, cherubically chubby man: Adlai Stevenson, Governor of Illinois.

Pressmen gathered around this figure who had established a growing reputation for wit, urbanity, articulateness, and—style. Did he want the nomination? he was asked.

His answer was no. "I am still a candidate for Governor of Illinois and nothing else."

Would he try to get the nomination?

His answer was no.

Would he accept if nominated? [1]

"I'll cross that bridge when I come to it," he replied.

Who was this man to whom the press turned almost by involuntary reflex? What qualifications had he for the Presidency? What were the sources of the warmth and magic that emanated from him and drew men

---

[1] In 1953, Stevenson wrote about this question, which was asked him many times from April to July 1952: ". . . If I said, 'Yes,' publicly or covertly, it would start the draft movement in earnest. If I said, 'No,' how would it reconcile with all my preaching about public service and politics? How could I foretell then, long before the convention, what manner of deadlock and bitterness might develop to the lasting damage of my party? And, finally, could anyone in good health and already in public life refuse the greatest honor and greatest responsibility in our political system? So I concluded to keep still and say nothing more to anyone, contenting myself with confidence that no one could in fact be drafted by a modern convention against his often-expressed wish. As the convention approached, that is what I told everyone, while I busied myself with the formation of committees, preparing my program and campaigning for Governor." *Major Campaign Speeches of Adlai E. Stevenson 1952* (New York: Random House, 1953), p. xxii.

to him wherever he appeared publicly? By what road had he traveled? What had he gathered along the way?

This is not the place for a full answer to these questions, but by way of perspective what follows may be a useful introduction to the man.

Adlai Stevenson was born to politics and American history. His great-grandfather on his mother's side was Jesse Fell, a founder of the Republican Party, close friend and one of the early Illinois advocates of Abraham Lincoln for the Republican nomination in 1860. His paternal grandfather, Adlai Stevenson, was elected Vice-President with Grover Cleveland in 1892. He was nominated again with William Jennings Bryan in 1900, and was a strong candidate for governor of Illinois in 1908. And his father, prominent in Illinois Democratic politics, served for a time as Secretary of State for Illinois.

His family had had a prominent part in making American history, and Adlai Stevenson had had around him in his youth at Bloomington, Illinois, history-makers of his family, their friends who had shared great adventures with them, the books, records, souvenirs of several crowded decades of our national life.

Stevenson is master of a distinguished writing style: witty, pungent, humorous, clear; and, when occasion demands, effectively sharp. Free, moreover, of the pomposities of prose that make the pronouncements of some of our officials sound like the suckings of leaky bilge pumps, he is often given to deprecation of himself and an occasional whimsey. In his famous message to the Illinois legislature vetoing a bill that

would have prevented cats from roaming at will, he
is seen at his lighthearted, refreshing, humane best:

. . . I cannot agree that it should be the declared public policy of Illinois that a cat visiting a neighbor's yard
or crossing the highway is a public nuisance. It is in the
nature of cats to do a certain amount of unescorted roaming. . . .

We are all interested in protecting certain varieties of
birds. That cats destroy some birds, I well know, but I believe this legislation would further but little the worthy
cause to which its proponents give such unselfish effort.
The problem of cat versus bird is as old as time. If we
attempt to resolve it by legislation, who knows but what
we may be called upon to take sides as well in the age-old
problems of dog versus cat, bird versus bird, even bird
versus worm. In my opinion, the state of Illinois and its
local governing bodies already have enough to do without
trying to control feline delinquency.

This same man, however, is capable of a Cromwel-
lian sternness, a quality deriving from his essentially
ascetic character, whatever his outward cavalier man-
nerisms. The sternness of this politically courageous
man, his sense of the need to be vigilant against the
freedom-constricting pressures of our times, appear
in his message to the Illinois legislature on June 26,
1951 vetoing a bill that, among other things, would
have established an "anti-subversive squad" to police
the state:

. . . We must fight traitors with laws. We already have
the laws. We must fight falsehood and evil ideas with
truth and better ideas. We have them in plenty. But we
must not confuse the two. Laws infringing our rights and

intimidating unoffending persons without enlarging our security will neither catch subversives nor win converts to our better ideas. And in the long run evil ideas can be counteracted and conquered not by law but only by better ideas.

. . . I know that to veto this bill in this period of grave anxiety will be unpopular with many. But I must, in good conscience, protest against any unnecessary suppression of our ancient rights as free men. Moreover, we will win the contest of ideas that afflicts the world not by suppressing these rights, but by their triumph. . . .

In outward appearance there is little to distinguish Stevenson from the ruck of his fellow citizens. Nor is there about him any of the Roman-senator look that occasionally marks our prominent public men, like, say, President Harding.

But he is a complex man. Free of the affectations of the professional politician, he is friendly but no backslapper, no hand-pumper or baby-kisser. Warm but not gushing, plain but not corny, he is devoted to the life of reason and scornful of the ways of demagoguery. His Presidential campaign, with its theme of talking sense to the American people, revealed to the nation his dedication to reason.[2]

[2] Writing in 1953 about the Presidential campaign, he said: "For years I have listened to the nauseous nonsense, the pie-in-the-sky appeals to cupidity and greed, the cynical trifling with passion and prejudice and fear; the slander, fraudulent promises, and the all-things-to-all-men demagoguery that are too much a part of our political campaigns. Sometimes in the deafening clamor of political salesmanship, I've thought that the people might be better served if a party purchased a half hour of radio and TV silence during which the audience would be asked to think quietly for themselves.

"Politicians all applaud and support public education as democracy's great monument and cornerstone, but does the politician,

But long before this, he had been quick to criticize reckless political statements and to oppose demagoguery. He said in Chicago on December 13, 1951:

. . . "McCarthyism" has become the trademark of a new breed of political demagogue who frightens the people with epithets, carelessly impugns the loyalty of patriotic men and shouts dire forebodings of a treacherous doom for America and all her cherished institutions. It is sad that America, at the height of her power, influence and well-being, should be ringing with slander, epithet, ill temper and the counsels of political desperation when all the world looks to us for dignity, sanity and confident leadership.

. . . And there are some words uttered by the first Republican which reckless politicians could well ponder. Abraham Lincoln said: "In times like the present, men should utter nothing for which they would not willingly be responsible through time and eternity." Not only in times like the present, but at all times, we should do noth-

---

the agent and spokesman of democracy, have no responsibility for public education? Government by the consent of the governed is the most difficult system of all because it depends for its success and viability on the good judgments and wise decisions of so many of us. But judgment and decision depend on information and understanding. In matters of public policy, candidates then have the greatest responsibility of all to inform truthfully, so that the people will understand and will have the tools of good judgment and wise decision. . . .

"I have no regrets about losing the election, except for the disappointment of so many dedicated supporters who share my hope of revitalizing a basic assumption of democracy: honest political leadership that despises the easy road to popularity and insists on focusing attention on reality and truth, however distasteful. Unless the great political parties and their spokesmen assume responsibility for educating and guiding the people with constant candor, how can we be sure that majority rule will meet the test of these searching times?" Ibid., pp. xxiv–xxv, xxx.

ing for which we would not wish to be held accountable in the future. The responsibility for our moral standards rests heaviest upon the men and women in public life, because public confidence in the integrity of the government is indispensable to faith in democracy. . . .

Free of the Presbyterian rigidity that marked Woodrow Wilson, Adlai Stevenson is a moralist without being priggish. He is deeply concerned over the fact that too many people scorn politics and public service. He told the graduating class of McKendree College in May 1952:

Help break the unhealthy habit that Americans have of using the word politics as an epithet, and of looking on all people in public life with suspicion or worse. . . .

I urge you to get into politics because the standards of Government must be raised and respect for public servants increased. When men and women in public life are selfish, unfair or unprincipled in their handling of the people's business they poison the very heart of our system.

Betrayers of public trust deserve the condemnation of their fellow citizens, but do not make the mistake of condemning all public men for the spectacular sins of the few. . . .[3]

[3] Writing in 1953, Stevenson mentioned that in 1943, "Somewhere, there in Italy, I think, I read about a public-opinion poll which reported that some seven out of ten American parents disapproved their sons going into politics or public service, or something like that. From what I had already seen of the war at home, in the Pacific, in the Mediterranean and from what I was still to see in Europe, I've often thought of that little morsel of news: fight, suffer, die, squander our substance, yes; but work in peacetime for the things we die for in war, no! There seemed to me something curiously inconsistent about the glorious, eager, uncomplaining sacrifices of war for the security of our homeland and its cherished institutions, and the active distaste of so many respectable people for peacetime participation in the politics and service of that homeland and its in-

As Governor of Illinois he was deeply concerned over the citizens' lack of interest in state government. A firm believer in strong, efficient states, he believed there should be less emotional talk about states' rights and more hard, resolute action to make state governments responsible and effective.

Born in the Lincoln country, absorbing Lincoln through his pores, hearing talk and reminiscences of Lincoln from his family, he has undoubtedly been deeply influenced by him. It was quite in character for Stevenson in his statement conceding the election to Dwight Eisenhower to tell the following Lincoln story to the group at his campaign headquarters: "Someone asked me, as I came in, down on the street, how I felt, and I was reminded of a story that a fellow-townsman of ours used to tell—Abraham Lincoln. They asked him how he felt once after an unsuccessful election. He said he felt like a little boy who had stubbed his toe in the dark. He said that he was too old to cry, but it hurt too much to laugh."

A graduate of Princeton University in 1922, widely read, widely traveled, with diplomatic experience through his services in the Department of State, avidly curious, intellectually and physically energetic, Stevenson is a modern man clinging to the ancient wisdom and old moralities.

After completing college he worked for the Bloom-

---

stitutions. Die for them—yes; work for them—no. Small wonder, I thought, that our 'politics' is no better, and great wonder that it is as good as it is. It seems to me sad that 'politics' and 'politician' are so often epithets and words of disrespect and contempt, and not without justification, in the land of Jefferson and in a government by the governed." Ibid., p. xviii.

ington *Pantagraph*, studied law at Northwestern University, and practiced law in Chicago from 1927 to 1933. Then he joined the Agricultural Adjustment Administration in Washington as a special counsel. Later that same year he was "loaned" to the Federal Alcohol Control Administration, an agency established to regulate the alcoholic-beverage industries until permanent legislation was forthcoming. After nearly a year in this work, he returned to law practice in Chicago.

The law and foreign affairs were his abiding interests in the next few years. In 1940 he headed the Chicago activities of the William Allen White Committee to Defend America by Aiding the Allies. He spent much of his time addressing meetings about the sinister threat of Hitler and Fascism and the need for aid to the Allies.

In July 1941 his old friend Colonel Frank Knox, the Secretary of the Navy and a Republican, asked Stevenson to join him in Washington as his Special Assistant and Counsel. His duties were varied and included travels to many theaters of war. In the fall of 1943 Colonel Knox "loaned" him to head an economic mission to survey the economic situation in Italy behind the Allied lines. A year later he visited England, France, and Belgium as a member of an Air Force mission. He has written:

They used to say that if you worked in wartime Washington, you would get one of three things: galloping frustration, ulcers or a sense of humor. I guess I got them all and I also got a great education in war, the world, our Government and my fellow man under every sort of trial and tension, from Congressional investigations to that shattering evening in the Secretary of the Navy's office while the news from Pearl Harbor was coming in. But I think my most intensive postgraduate education commenced that day I entered the State Department as Assistant to the Secretary, late in February, 1945.[4]

At the United Nations Conference at San Francisco, Stevenson served as press spokesman for the American delegation. He was appointed as a deputy to Edward R. Stettinius, Jr., with the rank of Minister, on the Preparatory Commission of the United Nations, which met in London in the autumn of 1945. When Stettinius fell ill, he became chief of the American delegation. Columnist Edgar Ansel Mowrer wrote that he did "what most representatives of foreign countries here consider a magnificent job."

When the first General Assembly of the U.N. met in London in January 1946, Stevenson was senior adviser to the American delegation, which included Secretary of State James Byrnes, Edward R. Stettinius, Jr., Eleanor Roosevelt, Congressman Sol Bloom, and Senators Tom Connally and Arthur Vandenberg. He was appointed by President Truman as an alternate delegate to the second U.N. session in the autumn of 1946. Reappointed for the 1947 sessions at Lake Success, he has written that this experience "confirmed with finality misgivings I had sorrowfully expressed early in 1946 about Russian intentions and our hopes for future tranquility."

Not only was he early alert to the threat of Soviet imperialism, but he also was sensitive to the aspirations

[4] Ibid., pp. xix–xx.

and struggles of the peoples of the Middle East and
Asia for a better way of life. The United States, he
knew, would be faced with many difficulties in working with these peoples just throwing off the last
vestiges of Western imperialism. The revolution
shaking Asia would require patience, tolerance, and a
sympathetic understanding on our part, particularly
if we wished to retain the friendship of uncommitted
nations like India.

When he returned to Chicago in December 1947,
the Democrats, under the leadership of Colonel
Jacob Arvey, asked him to run for governor. To the
question why did he agree to run, he has written: "I
don't know exactly; perhaps it was because of Father
and Grandfather Stevenson and Great-Grandfather
Fell who had all served Illinois; perhaps it was rest-
lessness about settling down again after eight feverish
years of war and peace; perhaps it was the encouragement of some determined friends . . . and perhaps
the public-opinion poll I saw in Italy had something
to do with it." [5]

After a few speeches by candidate Stevenson, *Time*
said that "veteran Chicago newsmen knew that a
dazzling new political star had been born." On election day, he was swept to victory by the largest
majority in Illinois history—572,000. He carried every
ward in Chicago and 48 of the remaining 101 counties
in this normally Republican state. Although one house
of the legislature was Republican-controlled during
his first two years and both houses had a Republican
majority in his last two years, he skillfully achieved

[5] Ibid., p. xx.

many improvements in state government. His accomplishments included:

Bringing top-level experts into high administrative posts regardless of political affiliation.

Removing the state police from political control and placing it under a merit system.

Doubling state aid to schools.

Greatly improving the state welfare program, with better care and treatment in the state mental institutions.

Streamlining the state financial system, improving the budgeting system and reorganizing state purchasing.

Launching the state's biggest road-reconstruction program with increases in the gas tax and truck-license fees to provide the funds.

Winning the first major battle for reforming the antiquated eighty-two-year-old state constitution.

Time said in the issue of January 28, 1952: "Stevenson looks and acts more like a hurrying, harried diplomat than a politician. Nearing 52, he has earned a small tendency to paunch and jowl, but he still gives the impression of slightness, and he is light enough on his feet to play a fair game of tennis. His manner is lawyerlike, earnest and—sometimes patiently, sometimes anxiously—engaging. He has a rueful laugh, nervous and sudden, a tongue in his head and a head on his shoulders."

For all his debonair manners and appearance of cavalier casualness, Stevenson is a careful, skillful politician, respectful of the uses of the craft. While believing in the importance of the party structure, he realizes that the party must continually adapt itself to the changing times to continue to fill its historic role of aiding the well-being and freedom of all the people. As Governor he demonstrated that service to the citizens, candor and a willingness to act responsibly in educating and guiding the people took precedence over service to the party.

This briefly, then, is the man around whom reporters swarmed on that night of March 29 in Washington, and who went on to receive the Democratic nomination for the Presidency in a manner unprecedented in our political history. He conducted a campaign that, though he lost it, raised American political thinking to a high plane and bequeathed it certain enduring qualities. His campaign speeches—the speeches of the loser—became best-selling books in the United States and overseas.

CHAPTER II

LAUNCHING THE STEVENSON DRAFT: FEBRUARY TO JULY 14

No ONE will be able to say precisely when Adlai E. Stevenson was first seriously mentioned as a Presidential possibility. Some of his Illinois supporters made at least passing reference to the possibility after his landslide victory in 1948. But he became the focus of increasing nation-wide attention when the newspapers on January 24, 1952 reported that, at President Truman's invitation, he had spent the previous evening at Blair House. The papers speculated that the President had asked him to run for the Democratic nomination.

Several days after this meeting, *Time,* which had been preparing a Stevenson story, hit the newsstands with his picture on the cover and a three-page article about his career and success as Governor. The *Time* account said of the meeting with the President: "Whatever the truth behind the rumors, this much was evident: in a cold season for the Democrats, Adlai Stevenson is politically hot, and Harry Truman feels the need of a little warmth." [1]

[1] Stevenson told me in May 1953, when I was with him on his world trip, that President Truman had asked him to call at Blair House and, at this two-hour session on January 23, had urged him to run for the nomination. Stevenson explained to the President that he could run for only one office; that it was too late for anyone

While Stevenson's name was attracting widespread comment following this January meeting with the President, a group of us in Chicago decided to launch an Illinois Committee Stevenson For President. It

---

else to file for Governor, and, besides, he wanted to finish the ambitious program he had started in Illinois. The President urged him to think about it. Then, early in March, just before the President went to Key West, the White House phoned Stevenson suggesting that he come to Washington. Fearing that if the newsmen knew he had seen President Truman a second time, this would only increase speculation that he was a candidate, the Governor was driven in a car with nonofficial license plates to the St. Louis airport by a state policeman in civilian clothes. He traveled under the name of William McCormick Blair, Jr., his administrative assistant. En route the commercial plane stopped at Louisville, Kentucky, where Stevenson's old friend Barry Bingham of the *Courier-Journal* had been alerted to meet him. Bingham told me on April 13, 1954: "I argued, with as much force as the brief period allowed, my conviction that he should not fight against a fate which seemed to have settled upon him. I did not urge him at all to make himself a candidate, or to promote his availability in any way at all. I only pleaded that he should leave himself uncommitted, so that a genuine draft could have an opportunity to develop. . . . As to his personal qualifications, I urged that the Democratic delegates and the people of the country in general should be allowed to judge for themselves on the basis of his public record. I contended that this was not a question of people being swept away by the force of a personality, but that there had been a genuine response to the qualities of leadership he had shown in his public utterances and to his progressive record as Governor of Illinois. In such a critical time, I argued, with a war going on in Korea and much confusion of purpose in America, it would be unjust for a man to refuse to serve in the highest office if his countrymen believed him capable of holding it. . . . He seemed worried, reluctant, and unwilling to admit that he could possibly be the only logical candidate for the Democratic nomination. . . . He was still refusing to acknowledge at this point that he could be nearly so serious a figure in American public life as his admirers were insisting that he was. . . . He was modest, friendly, deprecating, seeking advice and yet protesting that he could not bring himself to take it. As we parted, he laughed and said: 'Well, you certainly haven't been much help to me.'" When Stevenson saw President Truman, he repeated that he could run for only one office—Governor of Illinois. He could not, therefore, be a candidate for the Democratic nomination.

was our hope to set fire to the Stevenson talk around the country and also to demonstrate to the nation the high regard citizens of Illinois had for their Governor.

Illinois knew by February 1952 of Stevenson's unusual ability, his sensitive understanding of complex issues, his deep spiritual qualities, his humility, his essentially moderate attitude, and his keen sense of humor.

It was clear to those of us who organized the Illinois Committee that Stevenson was the ideal—and in fact the only—leading Democrat who could appeal to the many elements in the Democratic Party. The other prospective nominees of the Democratic Party—Senators Estes Kefauver, Richard Russell, and Robert Kerr, and later Averell Harriman—never were able to surmount the obstacle of seeming to have the support of only specific factional groups. Stevenson, on the other hand, had already demonstrated in Illinois that he was a successful leader of the group coalitions that form each of our two major parties. And, at the same time, he had proved he could win the support of independents for his program.

Many of us who organized the Illinois Committee had served or were serving as directors of the Independent Voters of Illinois. The I.V.I. for the past nine years had been a growing political force in Chicago politics. Composed of volunteer workers who ring doorbells at election time, it has considerable power in a number of wards of the city. Organized in 1943 to promote better candidates for office regardless of party affiliation, it has supported mainly Democrats nationally, but in local politics it has supported a number of Republicans. When Americans for Democratic Action was organized, the I.V.I. became the A.D.A. affiliate in Illinois. But the I.V.I. retained its autonomy of action. Its independence from the A.D.A. was manifested in the months prior to July 1952 by its interest in Stevenson for President when most of the A.D.A. leaders were for Harriman or Kefauver.

Early in February an executive committee was formed with George Overton, lawyer, and myself as co-chairmen. Richard Eiger, real-estate agent, served as treasurer, and Paul H. Berger, a business man, as secretary. The rest of the original executive committee consisted of lawyers Marshall Holleb, Hubert Will, Donald Petrie, and Edgar Bernhard; business man Richard A. Meyer; community newspaper publisher Leo A. Lerner; advertising men Irving J. Rosenbloom and Robert Knapp; public-relations counselor Mary S. Anderson; and Gwen Glasser, housewife.[2]

From the outset we adopted the policy of functioning separately from the I.V.I. as a broadly based citizens' movement. We had complete autonomy, being independent of the I.V.I. or any other group. We were simply and solely an organization of citizens unhindered by commitments to anyone.

In the days immediately following our organization, we secured as sponsors many citizens who never had been associated with the I.V.I.[3] As the Democratic

[2] Petrie and Knapp dropped off the committee sometime before the Democratic Convention.

[3] See, for instance, the list of sponsors in the *Chicago Sun-Times*, February 21, 1952, p. 41.

Convention approached, lawyers Maurice Rosenfield, Joseph Solon, and W. R. Ming, Jr., and Robert Klein, assistant to the Director of the Illinois Department of Public Welfare—all non-members of I.V.I.—were added to our executive committee, and also Congressman Sidney Yates, an I.V.I. member.

Early in February, volunteer workers called on many citizens in their homes to secure their names as sponsors of the Illinois Committee, and we sent the following letter to a selected list of people:

Dear Friend:

Do you want Adlai E. Stevenson to run for President?

The Illinois Committee for Stevenson for President has been formed, and is mobilizing support to draft him.

Although Governor Stevenson is not a candidate for President at this time, we believe that he could not refuse a genuine call from the American people, which we think should begin in Illinois.

Here's what you can do about it now.

Join the Committee as a sponsor. Give your moral and some modest financial support.

Fill out the enclosed card and mail it right away. Let's have an avalanche of favorable replies!

Then on February 21 we ran a full-page advertisement in the *Chicago Sun-Times* announcing the launching of the Draft Stevenson movement, printing a list of our sponsors, and urging others to join our ranks.

We decided quite early in our planning not to enter Stevenson's name in any primaries or encourage anyone else to do so. And we publicly repudiated an attempt to persuade people to write-in his name in the Illinois primary. Our conception of the committee's role was that we should prepare and distribute literature and Stevenson buttons, attract newspaper, radio, and television coverage, and stimulate people throughout the country to organize local Stevenson clubs. Our role at this point was educational —to acquaint the nation-wide public with Stevenson's record.

We corresponded with many people all over the country and sent them literature and buttons. We prepared a four-page brochure about Stevenson, which remained our major piece of literature until he received the nomination. This pamphlet was sent to editors and columnists, to Democratic congressmen, senators, and governors, and to Democratic state chairmen and National Committee members.

After explaining his background and record as Governor, the brochure carried on the last page the following statements of what was being said about him:

FORT WORTH STAR-TELEGRAM: By any standard of comparison, Gov. Stevenson has been an outstanding state executive. He has introduced businesslike administration into a state government which previously has been notably lax in its methods. His performance as governor has been honest and able . . . the United States can ill afford to lose the services of a public official of his demonstrated competence and integrity.

ALSOPS, NEW YORK HERALD TRIBUNE: The country desperately needs a dignified and sane debate of all the great issues confronting us . . . if such a man as Governor Stevenson is the Democratic candidate, Senator McCarthy himself will have a hard time getting away from the great issues, and dragging our politics back into the morass in which we are now floundering.

ARTHUR KROCK FROM WASHINGTON, IN THE NEW YORK TIMES: As Governor [Stevenson] has given Illinois an admirable and clean administration, after succeeding to a mess.

. . . ST. LOUIS POST-DISPATCH: A governor's ability may be judged not only by the legislation he signs, but by the bills which he prevents from becoming law. In either respect, Gov. Adlai E. Stevenson has done remarkably well. His 141 vetoes are a record which Illinois can view with gratitude.

CHRISTIAN SCIENCE MONITOR: Governor Stevenson . . . has a record of service, including action against corruption in government, which the Democrats, now on the defensive, can cite with justified pride.

NEW YORK HERALD TRIBUNE: Governor Stevenson has made an unusual record in Illinois for ability, integrity and range of vision; and a record, also, for gaining and keeping the confidence of the electorate in a state where the professionals of politics were at best lukewarm.

BY MARQUIS CHILDS FROM WASHINGTON: As governor, Stevenson has done a remarkable job, in spite of very great handicaps, cleaning up a mess left behind by a notorious Republican machine. This has, above all, been on the side of clean government. . . .

In addition to the brochure, we distributed copies of Bernard De Voto's "Stevenson and the Independent Voter" from *Harper's Magazine* of April 1952, and the February 18 issue of the *New Republic*, which published Stevenson's views on many issues. Since we were almost always out of money, we had to mimeograph these items rather than print them. Volunteers did the work, and occasionally they had to bring in paper and stamps for the operation to function.

Never knowing whether Stevenson would issue a statement like General Sherman's that he would refuse to run if nominated, the buttons we issued had just "Stevenson" on them so that they might at least be useful in the gubernatorial election. In case a Sherman-like statement materialized, we also had decided that any excess funds we might have would go to the Stevenson for Governor Committee.

From the time of the launching of our committee in February through to his receiving the nomination in July, we had no connection with the Governor. We were not acting as a front for him, nor did we ever receive any encouragement from him. Our sole encouragement—and it was mighty disheartening at times—was what any newspaper reader knew, that although he had come close to it, he had never said he would refuse to run if nominated.

We went on the assumption—with no such assurance from Stevenson himself—that he felt so strongly that citizens should take a more active interest in politics that he would be unable to ask us to cease our work. We believed that this was quite a different question from his request that Illinois party officials cease any efforts on his behalf as his declared purpose and prior party responsibility was to run for re-election as governor.

From time to time, and particularly after we had

opened Convention headquarters at the Conrad Hilton Hotel, individuals claiming to be close to Stevenson and to speak for him approached us. We generally ignored them. And we did not clear anything with such people. When one of them got in contact with several members of our committee early in July and said that Stevenson did not want us to open headquarters at the Hilton, we replied that we would not open our headquarters only if he issued a Sherman-like statement or made the request to us himself.

I, personally, did not talk to Stevenson from April 16 to July 26. On April 16 he phoned me on a problem related to state government. Our committee's efforts to draft him were not mentioned and I have subsequently heard that he knew little or nothing about them. Although I had known Stevenson since 1940, our friendship was casual. During his term as Governor I had seen him only occasionally; and a number of the other members of our executive committee had never even met him. During these months prior to the Convention his closest friends were heading the Stevenson for Governor Committee.

While our Draft Committee was at work in February and March stimulating interest in Stevenson, scores of newspapermen visited Springfield, and his name became more and more featured in the news. Prominent individuals in the party and a number of leading citizens also visited Springfield to try to persuade him to run. One day after his airplane had had difficulty landing through the Chicago fog, he said to reporters: "Flying around in fog is nothing new to me. I have had to answer more questions in the last

month than the Quiz Kids and Mr. Anthony put together." [4]

During this period he steadfastly refused to allow
his name to be entered in any primaries. When it
was entered in the Oregon primary without his permission—and when there was no legal way he could
have it withdrawn—he asked the Democrats of Oregon not to vote for him. Instead he urged Oregon
Democrats to vote for Senator Kefauver, the only
other Democrat entered in the Oregon primary.

The day after the Jefferson-Jackson Day dinner on
March 29, when President Truman's announcement
that he would not be a candidate caught the audience
by surprise, Stevenson appeared on *Meet the Press*.
May Craig, of the Portland, Maine, *Press-Herald*,
asked him whether he would say he would not accept
the nomination. He answered: "I will not say that. I
will say that that's a bridge that I can't cross until I
come to it and I see very little likelihood that I will
have to come to it."

Later in the TV program Stevenson said: "The

[4] *New York Times*, April 5, 1952. Stevenson wrote in 1953:
"All winter and spring people were coming to Springfield and tele-
phoning from all over the country—newspapermen, columnists, commentators, political leaders, friends, leaders of organizations, etc.,
etc. The mail became a real burden. First it was exhortation to announce my candidacy and enter primaries—'fight for the nomination.' To all, my explanation was the same: I was a candidate for
Governor of Illinois; I was committed to run for that office and one
could not run for two offices at the same time in good conscience, or
treat the highest office within the gift of the people of Illinois as a
consolation prize. Moreover, as the executive head of a huge business, the State of Illinois, I had little time to go around the country
campaigning for an unwanted nomination for an unwanted office—
an office, moreover, of such appalling difficulty and responsibility
in the year of grace, 1952, that I felt no sense of adequacy."

answer is just what I have said repeatedly and that is that I am pledged to run for Governor. I must run for Governor. I want to run for Governor. I seek no other office. I have no other ambition."

His able performance in answering the issues under discussion only added, however, to the growing talk that he was the man for the nomination. And the persistence of the reporters to get him to say he would or would not accept the nomination continued to focus the Presidential spotlight on him.

Newspaper speculation about him during the next few days became intense.[5] *Life* for March 24 had already appeared with his picture along with those of Kefauver, Russell, and Kerr on the cover. *Collier's* for April 19 ran a story entitled "Democrats' Dark-horse"; *Newsweek* for April 14 carried his picture on the cover with the caption "The Reluctant Candidate," and had a three-page story on his career; and *U.S. News & World Report* for April 25 published a seven-page interview with him about his stand on domestic and international issues.[6]

On April 1, three days after the Jefferson-Jackson Day dinner, we changed our name from the Illinois Committee to the National Committee Stevenson For President. We now tried more actively to stimulate Stevenson clubs in other parts of the country and

---

[5] See, for instance, the Alsop column, April 1; the *New York Times*, April 3, 6, 7, 11; *Chicago Daily News*, April 4, 10; *St. Louis Post-Dispatch*, April 6.

[6] The *Saturday Evening Post* on June 28 published an article by Joseph Alsop on Stevenson entitled "He'd Rather Not Be President"; *Look*, June 3, carried an article by Stevenson on "The States: Bulwark against 'Big Government'"; and the *Atlantic Monthly* in February had published his "Who Runs the Gambling Machines?"

weld them together into a centralized movement.[7]
We told the press about the many letters, telegrams,
and phone calls we had received the preceding two
days and said that "the wave of Stevenson sentiment
in the last 48 hours has confirmed the Committee's
belief of the popular support for the governor."

But "the wave of Stevenson sentiment" received
an almost fatal blow on April 16. On that spring day,
after having been renominated for Governor in the
primary eight days before, Stevenson took a determined step to remove himself from the Presidential
race. He issued this statement:

I have been urged to announce my candidacy for the
Democratic nomination for President, but I am a candidate for Governor of Illinois and I cannot run for two
offices at the same time. Moreover, my duties as Governor
do not presently afford the time to campaign for the nomination even if I wanted it.

Others have asked me merely to say that I would accept
a nomination which I did not seek. To state my position
now on a prospect so remote in time and probability seems
to me a little presumptuous. But I would rather presume
than embarrass or mislead.

In these somber years the hopes of mankind dwell with
the President of the United States. From such dread responsibility one does not shrink in fear, self-interest or
humility. But great political parties, like great nations,

[7] Lacking the staff to implement the organizing of local clubs,
little was accomplished here. Groups existed in New York City,
Philadelphia, Pittsburgh, Seattle, and Tacoma with which we had
some correspondence. Some of these clubs issued Stevenson literature
on their own initiative. Others were organized independently, but
apparently ceased after April 16. (See the *Seattle Times*, March 30;
New York Times, April 5; *New York Post*, July 25.)

have no indispensable man, and last January, before I was ever considered for the Presidency, I announced that I would seek re-election as Governor of Illinois. Last week I was nominated in the Democratic primary. It is the highest office within the gift of the citizens of Illinois, and its power for good or evil over their lives is correspondingly great. No one should lightly aspire to it or lightly abandon the quest once begun.

Hence, I have repeatedly said that I was a candidate for Governor of Illinois and had no other ambition. To this I must now add that in view of my prior commitment to run for Governor and my desire and the desire of many who have given me their help and confidence in our unfinished work in Illinois, I could not accept the nomination for any other office this summer.

Better state government is the only sound foundation for our Federal system, and I am proud and content to stand on my commitment to ask the people of Illinois to allow me to continue for another four years in my present post.

I cannot hope that my situation will be universally understood or my conclusions unanimously approved.

I can hope that friends with larger ambitions for me will not think ill of me. They have paid me the greatest compliment within their gift, and they have my utmost gratitude.

The *New York Times* the next morning observed that Stevenson "seems effectively to have closed the door to his nomination." But the *Times* added: "Many people will regret Mr. Stevenson's decision, for he is the type of man that either party should be proud to have as its leader." The same day Arthur Krock pointed out in the *Times* that President

Truman's announcement at the Jefferson-Jackson Day dinner and Governor Stevenson's statement meant that the Democrats would have their first open convention in twenty years. "This is a very unusual year in Democratic politics," he concluded.

The day after Stevenson issued his statement he flew to New York City to be present at a Democratic dinner in honor of Averell Harriman. In view of this statement, he felt that he could attend the dinner not as a candidate for the presidential nomination, but to pay his respects to his old friend Harriman. As he had already issued the statement, he believed that his speaking there would not be misunderstood.

Stevenson's brief speech that night electrified the audience:

I am told that I am here at the head table by misrepresentation and fraud; that you invited a candidate for President but got a candidate for Governor instead. I feel like the weary old Confederate soldier, unarmed, ragged and asleep, whom some zealous young Union soldiers captured. "Git up, Reb, we got you now," they shouted. "Yeah," the old fellow said, "and it's a heck of a git you got."

. . . This year we must select a new President of the United States—as well as the old Governor of Illinois, I hope! The burdens of the Presidency dwarf the imagination. And the next President will have something more to face than most any of his predecessors—guidance toward coexistence in this world with a ruthless, inscrutable and equal power in the world. This is a new and fearsome position for the United States, and its President will be sorely tried.

Perhaps it isn't exactly the thing to say to a partisan

meeting, but who wins this fall is less important than what wins—what ideas, what concept of the world of tomorrow, what quality of perception, leadership and courage. . . .

We can be proud of our twenty years of faith and service in the American way. But we must look forward, not back. Rather we lose this election than mislead the people by representing as simple what is infinitely complex, or by representing as safe what is infinitely precarious. For there are no painless solutions to war, inflation, communism, imperialism, hunger, fear, intolerance, and all the hard stubborn problems that beset us.

And no living American knows more about them, or has given more wisdom, patience and relentless effort to their solution, at home and abroad, during the whole span of these two great decades than a great Democrat, your guest of honor, Averell Harriman.

The next day the *New York Post* remarked: ". . . the man who said he could not accept the presidential nomination . . . was the one speaker whose oratory, wit and liberal commentary evoked a spontaneous and prolonged response . . . the dinner for Harriman may come to be remembered as the starting point for a real draft-Stevenson movement."

In the weeks following the Harriman dinner, however, many who had been interested in promoting the Stevenson candidacy gave up hope. Many party leaders, puzzled over what was the orthodox step to take in this unorthodox situation, gradually abandoned the idea of drafting Stevenson. Many of them apparently felt that no man could be drafted for a party nomination without making pledges in advance. And Colonel Arvey has written that for the week after the Harriman dinner "I did my best to draw the Governor into the race, then I gave up." [8] He was quoted in the press as saying that it was unlikely the Convention would draft Stevenson. It would "almost take a miracle for it to happen," he observed. But he added that he was willing "to bet every dollar I have that if it happened the Governor couldn't turn it down." [9]

Many of the leaders of Americans for Democratic Action announced their support of Harriman's candidacy, while some actively supported Estes Kefauver. Apparently many of these independents were so professional that they needed to have a candidate to support at the earliest possible date.[1]

In spite of the fact that many abandoned hope that Stevenson could be made the nominee, our committee in Chicago refused to disband. We were, however, disheartened. At one discussion a majority seemed to favor ceasing our efforts, but Gwen Glasser, the housewife on our executive committee, said: "If we give up, who will be left? We're the last hope."

In continuing our efforts, we grasped at the fact that Stevenson had said he "could not accept the nomination for any other office this summer," *not* he *would not* accept the nomination for any other office.

Plans we had made early in April for a powerful national organization with field representatives had to be

[8] "The Reluctant Candidate—An Inside Story," *Reporter*, November 24, 1953.
[9] *New York Times*, April 20; p. E 3.
[1] Although the A.D.A. did not endorse any candidate at their annual convention in May, it was clear that the national leaders favored Harriman.

abandoned. These were difficult days financially for the committee. Anyone with experience in politics knows how difficult it is to raise money for a non-existent candidate. One of our few contributors wrote: "In view of our candidate's behavior, this may be the lost-est cause I have ever contributed to, but I want to uphold your good strong right arm in keeping the lamp burning for the only candidate that seems to have the necessary qualifications."

We had raised $4,280.52 up to mid-April, and from then until July 16 we were able to raise only $3,160.75 more. Nevertheless we had hired Miss Florence Medow on April 1—the only paid staff member until July 14, and part of the time she went without salary—and we kept the office going with ample volunteer help under the guidance of Miss Medow, Gwen Glasser, Co-chairman George Overton, and volunteer worker Dan Burkholder.

Although it was difficult to procure an appointment with Arvey, several times in May various members of our executive committee discussed the draft situation with him. Arvey stated that, at the expressed wish of the Governor, he was doing nothing to promote the candidacy other than answering his mail and phone calls. Yet he remarked that he was "astounded" at the way talk of drafting Stevenson continued to grow. The way the name Stevenson was booming, he said, "changes my whole experience in politics." He then read some of the pro-Stevenson letters that he had received. He added that if a draft did occur, he ex-pected it would happen after a deadlock. Then, he said, someone like Eleanor Roosevelt would address the deadlocked Convention and move the nomination of Stevenson.

No funds for our efforts and no real expression of encouragement ever came from these meetings with Arvey.

Although most party leaders had abandoned Stevenson as a candidate, the substantial volume of mail our office continued to receive every day—some of it from Convention delegates—pointed to the strong sentiment for him in many areas of the nation. We suggested to our correspondents that they write to Stevenson and urge him to accept the nomination. Meanwhile the newspapers continued to speculate about him, reporting that his mail was growing and that long-distance telephone calls were coming into Springfield with regularity.

During late April and May, Stevenson made a series of speeches in Texas, Oregon, and California— speeches that had been arranged early in January before talk of his Presidential candidacy had developed. At Dallas he reiterated his insistence that he was not a candidate, but again refused to answer questions whether he would accept a draft.

A few days later in Portland, when pressed by reporters to say whether he would accept a draft, he said:

I cannot speculate about hypothetical situations. But I don't believe there ever has been a genuine draft of an unwilling man for the presidential nomination by either party.

I doubt if such a thing is possible.

That is all I can say on this story—I regret that I cannot give you a good story.

When a reporter persisted in asking whether he wouldn't accept a draft, Stevenson smiled and replied: "Why don't you put that question in German? It has been put in every other language, it seems." [2]

Two days later in California, when newsmen asked him what he would say if the Convention attempted a draft, he replied: "I had better wait until the improbable arrival of that situation before I comment."

When asked if he was staying out of the Presidential race because he was "afraid" of running against General Eisenhower, he said: "I'm not afraid to run against Ike." Then, with a smile, he added: "I don't think Ike is afraid of me." [3]

When he arrived at the annual Conference of State Governors on June 30, he told reporters:

I have not participated, nor will I participate, overtly or covertly, in any movement to draft me. Without such participation on my part I do not believe any such draft can or will develop.

In the unlikely event that it does, I will decide what to do at that time in the light of the conditions then existing.

A few hours after this statement, Governor Henry F. Schricker of Indiana—who later became a key figure in the draft movement—told newsmen: "I'd say Governor Stevenson is definitely available. And I'd like to ask how any man could possibly turn down a sincere draft." [4]

But on July 12—the day the Republican Conven-

[2] *Chicago Sun-Times*, May 2.
[3] Ibid., May 4, 10.
[4] *Chicago Sun-Times*, July 1, 3.

tion closed—Stevenson's press officer issued this statement:

He is a candidate for re-election as Governor of Illinois, and as he has often said, wants no other office. He will ask the Illinois delegation to continue to respect his wishes and he hopes all of the delegates will do likewise.

This statement seems to have completed the discouragement of many of the leaders of the party. By this time they seem to have given up hope of drafting Stevenson. As I have said, a draft to them apparently meant careful planning and assumed an agreement with the candidate to be drafted. No such agreement was forthcoming from Stevenson.

Newsweek for July 7 captured the discouragement of many party leaders:

Democratic leaders are beginning to fear that, if Stevenson doesn't speak out soon, a draft may become impossible.

. . . The Fair Deal leadership, therefore, had been exerting a steady and heavy pressure on Stevenson. Col. Jacob Arvey . . . and former Sen. Scott Lucas have transmitted the Administration's sense of urgency. They warn the Governor that he cannot wait for a spontaneous move by the delegates in Convention assembled. Should he hold off from any public avowal until that time, they warn, he may well lose by default.[5]

[5] Stevenson wrote in 1953: "Contrary to the impression of some, I had no understanding whatever with President Truman at any time that I was available. To set at rest still another rumor, I think my friend, Colonel Arvey, the National Committeeman from Illinois, would testify that during those six months I repeatedly urged him to do nothing in my behalf and repeatedly he assured me he neither had nor would, always adding that he was bedeviled with incessant pressures and inquiries." *Major Campaign Speeches of Adlai E. Stevenson,* p. xxiii.

Although Stevenson's July 12 statement shook some of the confidence of our committee, nevertheless we moved ahead with our Convention plans. But by now we had only about one hundred dollars of unspent money.

That day we completed the mailing of the following letter, over the signature of the two co-chairmen, to every delegate and alternate to the convention:

Dear Friend:

The Democratic Party *can* win in 1952!

But to do so it must nominate a candidate who represents the real aspirations of a majority of the American people.

Millions have joined the ranks of the party and voted for its leaders because of their desire for their own and their children's betterment and national safety. These hopes must not be betrayed.

Such a candidate must not only carry forward the program wanted by the people, but must also gain support for new efforts required by new circumstances.

The American people need in their next President a man of courage, patience and wisdom, whose knowledge covers the whole area of our national interests. This involves not only the ordinary business of making government serve people wisely at home, but also the more delicate task of piloting the nation through its greatest international crisis.

The United States is committed to meeting the challenge from powers who claim to offer a better way of life than ours. We cannot meet this challenge by military force alone. We must show that our way offers security and freedom.

The demonstration of our ability to improve the lot of

the common man will take a long time. It will demand patience, as well as resolution. These qualities exist in our people. They can find expression only if national leadership is equal to the task of meeting succeeding crises.

We stand committed, also, to a domestic program that calls for increased productivity both in industry and agriculture. It also calls for a fair income to all our people. This means high wages; it means support for agriculture; it means an adequate system of social security for the dependent, the aged, and the unemployed; it means educational opportunities, progress through research and encouragement for individual initiative.

Recognizing these responsibilities and realizing that leadership is so important, we believe that the man best suited to meet the challenge of our times should be the Democratic Party's candidate.

That man is Governor Adlai E. Stevenson of Illinois.

He was elected by the largest majority in the history of Illinois.

He has been a successful governor of the state. He has demonstrated that he knows how to get things done. He has reformed the state government, made it sensitive and responsible to people's needs, and economized its operation.

He has had wide experience as a diplomat in international matters; he recognizes the nature of the world crisis, and is more capable of meeting the issues it raises than any other suggested candidate of either party. He has shown repeatedly that he has a quick and comprehensive mind, is devoted to democracy, and has a wisdom and caution which would guard against military adventurousness.

We have no doubt Governor Stevenson, devoted as he is to public service, will respond to the call of higher duty and will accept the Democratic nomination for President.

You will be best serving the interests of your party and of the nation in casting your vote for the candidate most certain to be elected and whose career already promises that he will be one of the greatest Presidents in our history.

The National Committee Stevenson for President, a group of independent citizens, will have headquarters at the Conrad Hilton Hotel starting July 19th. Please drop in and see us. We look forward to meeting you.

We included with this letter a guide to Chicago, which we had obtained free from the Chamber of Commerce. We then stamped on the guide: "Stevenson for President!"

We ordered one thousand large round red, white, and blue "America Needs Stevenson For President" buttons. Paper badges with Stevenson's name were made. Kits of lapel buttons and literature were prepared. Volunteers had been working for days preparing a detailed card file of every delegate and alternate, containing all pertinent information about the voting plans of the delegate. A room with a direct phone was rented in the Stock Yards Inn next door to the Convention auditorium. And a number of telegrams were sent to key leaders urging them to join our draft movement.

On Saturday, July 12, we released an announcement to the press that we would open Convention headquarters on July 19, and added:

In many communities throughout the United States and in its territories independents, liberals, Democratic Party leaders, organizations and individuals have indicated a strong and growing interest in Stevenson as the Democratic candidate.

This movement has been entirely spontaneous and has not been associated with official members of the Democratic national organization. It has been financed by small contributions from people who admire Governor Stevenson, with some gifts being as low as 35 and 50 cents.

With very little money and no connection with officials of the Democratic party, a grass roots movement has developed all over the country that is now ready to swing behind Stevenson and work for his election when he becomes the candidate for President.

CHAPTER III

OPENING CONVENTION
HEADQUARTERS:
MONDAY, TUESDAY, WEDNESDAY,
JULY 14, 15, 16

ON MONDAY, July 14, many of the candidates for the Democratic nomination, their supporters, and officials of the Democratic National Committee flocked into Chicago to open campaign headquarters in hotel rooms just vacated the day before by the Republicans. And most of the newspaper, radio, and TV corps, after reporting the climax of the Republican Convention on Saturday the 12th, remained in Chicago to cover activities of the Democrats prior to their Convention.

Although we had intended to wait until Saturday the 19th to open quarters at the Hilton Hotel, the number of phone calls, telegrams, and visitors to our small office in the Chicago Loop so swamped our limited facilities that we quickly moved up our date for opening at the Hilton to Wednesday the 16th.

We said in a press release on July 15:

From the moment we announced last Sunday [the 13th] that the Committee was going ahead with a draft Stevenson campaign we have been amazed at the enthusiastic public response.

Despite Governor Stevenson's apparent refusal, the

country continues to say it needs him. We have received so many requests for information and offers of help, that we must open the Conrad Hilton headquarters four days early. Delegates from many states have written, wired and telephoned for information and an opportunity to meet with us and plan the draft Stevenson campaign. Never in the history of American politics has there been such a spontaneous upsurge for a man who is not an avowed candidate.

Typical of the letters and telegrams we were receiving was one from Arkansas which closed with: "Good luck, and may God bless your efforts."

One thing we were not blessed with at this point, as has been hinted, was money. But we had hundreds of enthusiastic volunteer workers. We quickly exhausted our one thousand big "America Needs Stevenson For President" buttons. We cautiously reordered two thousand more, and two days later another two thousand. And our mimeograph machine was kept running at full speed turning out copies of favorable newspaper stories about Stevenson and other campaign matter.

But our funds were so meager that on July 16 we rented only three hotel rooms—1500, 1501, and 1502. Reluctantly—preferring to spend our money on literature and buttons—we spent $170 to rent office furniture for these rooms. Three rooms adjoining ours were registered under our name, but their cost was underwritten by people friendly to our cause who agreed to allow us to use their rooms except when they were sleeping in them.

The many newspaper, radio, and TV reporters and delegates who came to see us on the day we opened forced us to rent two more rooms the following day. On Saturday the 19th the press for space led us to take over entirely the three adjoining rooms that had been lent us. By this time over three hundred delegates had come to see us.

Our expanding activities also required adding a few people to the payroll of one we had had until July 14.[1]

The mere opening of our Draft Stevenson headquarters attracted widespread newspaper comment. Newsmen were impressed by the enthusiasm of our volunteers and by the determination of our committee to push ahead in spite of the fact that we did not have our candidate's consent.

Paul Ringler, for instance, said in the *Milwaukee Journal* (July 21):

Committees with presidential candidates and toney headquarters are no novelty at this Democratic National Convention. They clutter up the place.

We give you, therefore, a Committee that is different. Almost fantastically different. It has no candidate. It has little money. It has headquarters of Spartan simplicity.

It is the National Committee Stevenson For President. It has headquarters on the 15th floor of the Conrad Hilton Hotel. It has enthusiastic leaders and a growing throng of ardent workers. It teems with enthusiasm.

But it has no candidate.

The man it backs, Gov. Adlai Stevenson of Illinois, keeps on insisting, as he has for months, that he is not a candidate for the nomination and doesn't want to be a candidate.

Yet the committee, unimpressed, uninfluenced and un-

---

[1] Our total payroll budget from March to September—when we closed our books—was $2,993.79.

awed, goes right on working just as if Stevenson were as much a candidate as Alben Barkley, Estes Kefauver, Richard Russell, Robert Kerr, etc.

It's not only confusing, it is amusing.

In the *Washington Star* (July 23), B. M. McKelway, after describing the various candidate headquarters in the Hilton, wrote:

On the 15th floor of the hotel is the most unusual headquarters of all. It has its buttons, its free soda pop, its volunteer ladies and young men who want to be most helpful. In such respects it is like all other headquarters. But unlike all the others it is manned by volunteers working in the interest of a man who declines to have anything to do with it, who avoids any direct or indirect liaison with those in charge of it.[2]

The fifteenth floor of the Hilton had been the headquarters of Governor Earl Warren during the Republican Convention. It had been quite an elaborate layout. But our original space requirements of three rooms directly off the foyer were only a fraction of the former Warren headquarters.

At the beginning we had only the house phones into this three-room suite. The Warren headquarters had set up a private switchboard in one of the smaller rooms. We had this removed, feeling that we could not afford it and that certainly we would never need it. How wrong we were! Two days after it had been removed, the telephone company had a crew back on

[2] For some other feature stories on the Draft Committee see *Boston Globe*, July 27; Watertown, N.Y., *Times*, August 8; *Belmont* [Chicago] *Booster*, August 10; *Newsweek*, August 4; *Hyde Park* [Chicago] *Herald*, August 6.

the fifteenth floor installing seven additional private lines in the expanded quarters. They also installed an intercommunication line between some of the "screening points" in the hallways.

People and volunteers? Hundreds were constantly milling around the foyer and workrooms. Our policy of no demonstrations or parades eliminated that outlet for their energies. At one point Dave Garwin, our communications expert, bought enough pasteboard and sign-painter's ink to keep them busy painting signs. Some of the slogans these volunteers thought up were classics. Volunteer workers are great people—the lifeblood of the democratic process in action!

We had one fear about our headquarters, and it was created by the Democratic Convention headquarters itself. Organized as they were along traditional lines, the Convention personnel continually turned to us for information about Stevenson's wishes, appointments, releases on his welcoming address, and invitations to be issued. It was efficiency on their part, certainly, but they could not get it into their heads that we were not representing Stevenson; we had no contact with him and certainly could accept nothing in his name or addressed to him. This was not only confusing; it was embarrassing.

So we decided that any communications for Stevenson such as mail, telegrams, or messages which came to the fifteenth floor would be delivered to the hotel floor clerk. And I wrote to the hotel management:

It has just come to my attention that mail and telegrams addressed to Governor Adlai Stevenson are being delivered to the National Committee, Stevenson For President.

We are not authorized to receive mail or telegrams for the Governor. The National Committee is independent of the Governor, and mail addressed to this Committee is all that we can receive.

We learned later that the hotel had an acute problem at the telephone switchboard, trying to sort out the calls that were intended for Stevenson from those which were intended for us. We learned later, too, that many who wanted to reach us never did. Those are the costs of such a hectic, tense, independent operation in connection with a political convention.

The climax of all this came on the final day of the Convention. Thousands of gladioli in huge tin tubs were delivered to the fifteenth floor. They were sent with good wishes to Stevenson from the wholesale gladioli-growers. They took up so much room in the foyer that there was no room for people. They created a traffic emergency, so we made arrangements to have them immediately sent to hospitals. We hope the thoughtful growers did not mind, and as the Convention was over, we advised a member of the Governor's staff that an appropriate acknowledgment was in order.

The executive committee of the Draft Stevenson Committee functioned as a working group throughout the days and nights from July 16 to July 26. Since Co-chairman George Overton had had to go to Europe on business, he was replaced by Leo A. Lerner as acting co-chairman. The two co-chairmen talked to the press, appeared on countless radio and TV programs, and met with many key delegates.[3]

Marshall Holleb and Hubert Will, with the assistance of Congressman Sidney Yates of Chicago's 9th Congressional district, and of W. R. Ming, Jr., of the University of Chicago Law School, were in charge of contacts with the delegates. Paul Berger, Alexander Pope, and Bernard Sachs were in charge of volunteers, assigning them a variety of tasks. Public relations were in charge of the late Stuart Haydon, an old friend I had asked to come from Washington to help us. He was assisted by Al Wiseman, Chicago public-relations man, and Mary S. Anderson and I. J. Rosenbloom of the executive committee. Office management was in charge of Florence Medow, Barbara Simpson, Constance Chadwell, and Mary Jane Krensky. Finances were handled by Richard N. Eiger, Maurice Rosenfield, and Robert Klein. David and Jean Garwin, and Ann Ewing from Washington, were in charge of communications and organization.

A service to monitor all radio and TV broadcasts as well as to clip all news stories was supervised by the late Mrs. Richard Eiger. These volunteers were mainly University of Chicago students who set for themselves a twenty-four-hour round-the-clock schedule. They read all the metropolitan papers of the country and summarized what was being written. Together with this, some of them covered all radio and TV outlets in Chicago. Any pertinent statements, observations, or in-

[3] See, for instance, "Can the Democrats Maintain Their Coalition," *The University of Chicago Round Table*, July 20, 1952.

terviews were phoned in to our headquarters and typed up for the executive committee.

Many of the news stories describing our activities at the Hilton placed great emphasis on our being amateurs. Robert L. Riggs, for instance, described us in the *Louisville Courier-Journal* as "a determined band of amateurs." And James Reston referred to us in the *New York Times* as "the greatest amateur show since Major Bowes."

We were amateurs in that we were not delegates to the Convention; we were not office-holders in the Democratic Party; and we had not participated in Presidential-convention politics before. But we were not amateurs in local and state politics. Almost everyone on our executive committee had, at some time, rung doorbells and asked citizens to vote for the candidates he was supporting. Moreover, some of us had had considerable experience in preparing campaign literature, organizing political headquarters, and making speeches on behalf of candidates.

Will, Holleb, and Ming—the three key members in charge of contacts with the delegates—had helped in campaigns for Congress, in City Council elections, and in campaigns for senatorial and house seats in the state legislature. They had also been active in the affairs of the American Veterans Committee, particularly at the A.V.C. national conventions.

Co-chairman Lerner had for years been a potent force in Chicago politics, particularly in those areas of the city where his community newspapers circulated. Joseph Solon, important in planning our over-

had been the campaign manager for sev-
ratic candidates for office.

lic-relations director, Stuart Haydon, had
director in the 1942 Illinois campaign for
tes senator, and he had had long experience
as a w... ng newsman for the *Chicago Daily News* and
the United Press, and since 1943 as a free-lance writer
in Washington. His contacts with the national press-
radio-TV corps proved to be invaluable in our activities.

I, too, had had political experience prior to 1952.
My mother had been the first woman to campaign for
the office of selectman in Nahant, Massachusetts. As
a youngster in that campaign, I remember checking
voting lists and getting people to the voting booth.

In Chicago I was a supporter of Paul H. Douglas
when he was in the City Council, and had actively
campaigned for him when he sought the Democratic
nomination for the United States Senate in 1942. The
next year I ran—unsuccessfully—for the post of alder-
man in the City Council against the opposition of
both the Republican and the Democratic organizations. A year later I took part in the campaign of Emily
Taft Douglas for congresswoman at large on the Democratic ticket. Then, in 1947, I was prominent in the
aldermanic race of Robert E. Merriam. Although I
was out of the state in the closing months of Stevenson's campaign for governor and Douglas's campaign
for senator, I had participated in the early phases of
these two campaigns.

Not only was the press fascinated by our amateur
standing in national politics, but there was much spec-

ulation in some papers about a possible connection between our Draft Committee and Jacob Arvey.

The relation between our committee and Arvey from July 16 to Stevenson's nomination can best be described as nonexistent. On a TV program on Tuesday, July 15—the day before we opened at the Hilton —Arvey rated the possibility of a Convention draft of Stevenson as "very, very slim." He was quite critical of our committee "for operating against the Governor's wishes," and Arvey said he had asked us to stop.

In the context of facts, Arvey's TV statement had a greater meaning for us than it did for his vast television audience. Incidentally, it was the first test run of our volunteer monitoring service. The complete text of his statement was phoned to me at the hotel room of Stuart Haydon just a few minutes after Arvey was off the air.

During dinner we had laid out our plan of press releases. We intended to release nothing but statements outlining our complete independence of any organization, clique, or group. We also planned to issue periodic reports of the numbers of delegates who had sought information and, when plausible, a tabulation of the votes for Stevenson when supported by a process of check and double check of what the delegates had told us.

Arvey's TV statement actually furnished us an early opportunity of establishing our independence from him or, for that matter, from anyone else.

This is the text of the statement we drafted in answer to the Arvey telecast:

Colonel Arvey's statement has just been called to my attention. I'm sorry, I didn't hear it myself. But if what is reported to me is what was said, I can only reply that it has never been in the province of his influence to tell us to do anything, much less disband or reorganize.

With regard to his reference to the Governor's wishes, he apparently ignores the fact that our Committee is Independent and represents the desire of thousands of citizens with the fervent conviction that Governor Stevenson should be nominated. The Governor knows this, consequently, the Governor would never be presumptuous enough to attempt to dictate the actions of independent citizens in our democracy.

Now, to say that all went smoothly within our group would be both untruthful and unfair; for ours was a group of people no more infallible and no more omnipotent than any other group of intensely interested citizens. This statement proved to be one cause for the first conflict that arose to face us, from perfectly normal differences of opinion within our committee. Several committee members argued that it would serve no good purpose to argue with Arvey.

It might be a natural political assumption, because we were Chicagoans and because Stevenson had specifically asked the Illinois delegation and its leaders to do nothing to foster his nomination, that the leaders of the Illinois delegation would find some way to do what they had been asked not to do and that we were the group. My prime purpose in this release, therefore, was to show that we were not a front for the Illinois delegation; that nothing could alter our effort. I felt that we should not leave any one of the many steps leading up to a genuine draft of Stevenson open to question. He should go before the country as a candidate with no political strings or promises attached.

We decided finally not to release our statement. Not releasing our statement lost us the opportunity to nip in the bud the charge that we were under the control of the Illinois delegation—a charge that is not yet completely dispelled.

Actually, the nearest Arvey ever came to asking us to stop our efforts was on Monday afternoon, July 14. Lerner and I were in a Hilton elevator. The door opened at the eighth floor. There were flags, bunting, and signs in the foyer, and we looked out to see whose headquarters were there. It proved to be those of the Democratic National Committee. Arvey, who was standing there, invited us to step out of the elevator. When we did, he asked: "What are you fellows doing around here?"

When we replied that we had just rented some rooms and were opening up on Wednesday, he expressed amazement and said: "I don't know what you are doing that for; Governor Stevenson is not a candidate."

At this point in the conversation a *Wall Street Journal* reporter tried to ask the colonel some questions about Stevenson. Arvey told him, as he walked away: "Ask these two, they seem to know more than I do."

Arvey's amazement at our renting rooms in the Hilton Hotel was quite understandable. First, Stevenson had instructed him that he was not a candidate.

Second, he knew that the Democratic National Committee had not allocated us space. When we first asked the Hilton for rooms, the management replied that all space was booked by the Democratic National Committee, through which, therefore, we would have to secure rooms. As we were unofficial and unrecognized by the Committee, we decided not to deal with it. Instead, working through friends, we persuaded the hotel management to rent us space directly.

Our relations with Stevenson, too, were nonexistent except for an exchange of telegrams on July 15. I received the following telegram at my home:

Have just seen circular letter to delegates and am very much disturbed in view of my unwillingness to be candidate. Have consistently avoided trying to influence your committee's activities feeling that my position was manifest and that I could not properly ask you to cooperate as a friend if your group had other views in conflict with my wishes. . . . I do not want to embarrass you and I am grateful for your good will and confidence but my attitude is utterly sincere and I desperately want and intend to stay on this job, with your help I hope. Regards. Adlai E. Stevenson.

It was another expression of his not seeking the nomination, which, of course, was not news. His sentence: "Have consistently avoided trying to influence your committee's activities feeling that my position was manifest and that I could not properly ask you to cooperate as a friend if your group had other views in conflict with my wishes," indicated as much.

Stuart Haydon and I drafted a reply in language that, if he should not answer, would imply he would not refuse a draft by the Convention. This gave a peculiar twist to logic: a negative (no reply) would become a positive (he would not refuse a nomination).

It was at this exact point that we developed a few new phrases in the political thinking of the moment. Everyone in the political arena had been asking: "Will he accept?" Newspapers, news magazines, radio and television commentators, all had been emphasizing the speculation over Stevenson's accepting the nomination. In our minds, the weight of the emphasis was in the wrong place.

The nomination, *per se*, was a decision for the Convention to make—not for Stevenson. If he had openly, and unequivocally, stated in simple words: "I will not accept the nomination, come hell or high water," the Convention could, if it wished, still nominate him. Aside from the point that it would make both Stevenson and the Convention look politically stupid, it was within the rights of each to say and do just that.

So the emphasis of "Will he accept?" connoted a situation that did not exist. In the ethical sense, for us, the question never was the dominance of Stevenson's wishes. Our sole contention was that the Convention, in the name of its party, should pick the man it decided offered the most for the nation's good.

We could only support our contention that Stevenson was the most able man by aiding the delegates in a full freedom of choice, based on the best information available and on an evaluation of the political realism of selecting a man with Stevenson's broad appeal. It was, in the best sense, the democratic process of "the office seeking the man," a philosophy long in disuse.

With his telegram in hand, we felt it an opportunity to put on record all these things as we had reasoned them out.

I felt sure that if he intended not to accept, he would make such an announcement—one which could bear that interpretation only. And I felt just as sure that his sense of the appropriate would not permit him to allow the Convention to nominate him and then face a refusal. Such an act toward his own political party would be unforgivable in view of his own philosophy of participation in public life, even though he could point to the consistency of his saying that he did not wish to be a candidate for the nomination.

What he had said was that he did not wish to be a candidate for the nomination, which is quite different from saying that he would not accept if nominated by the Convention.

I wired back to Springfield:

. . . Regarding Committee; we are and intend only to reflect the will of the people in the best interest of not only the Democratic Party, but of the nation. We feel it our duty to answer thousands of requests from all across the country to furnish information about you together with synopsis of your stated position on various topics and your record as Governor. When a responsible proportion of such requests began coming in from delegates, and continue to even this very hour, we feel we can do nothing other than what we are doing and be fair to the thousands of people who have no other source. Our present intention is to be that of an information center. Should this become a draft movement on the part of those who sincerely, honestly, and fervently want you as their candidate, that is democracy in its purest action. Neither you nor I should or would ever question the right of a voter to fight to the last ditch for the man he thinks should win. Believe me, we both must be governed by our sincerity of purpose and history will record the result. My highest regards. Walter Johnson.

One other Stevenson contact did occur—not with Adlai E. Stevenson, but with his sons John Fell and Borden Stevenson. On Saturday, July 19, John Fell suddenly appeared, getting off an elevator on the fifteenth floor of the Hilton, wearing one of our large "America Needs Stevenson For President" buttons. We quickly took him and an accompanying friend from the foyer to one of our private rooms.

John Fell was sixteen years old. He seemed quite concerned about what was being done to his father. It was not simply curiosity; it was genuine concern.

At first his young friend did most of the talking and gave those of us present quite a lecture on the greatness of the Republican Party—and particularly of Senator Taft. Some of this amused John Fell, and his young friend amused even himself.

John Fell, in answer to our question why he had come up to the fifteenth floor, said he wanted to see the people who were trying to make his father do what he said he did not wish to do.

We explained that a great number of sincere citizens were of the belief his father would make a good President. We likened this to the belief and confidence that he, as a son, had in his father. We also explained that we believed his father had proved himself to have the qualities that our form of government needs and honors.

John Fell asked some questions—not many. But those he did ask seemed to reflect a groping for understanding of a situation that had suddenly, and dramatically, affected his own life.

We then explained to him that from his own presence in our headquarters certain inferences were possible. And we prepared for his exit by sending a few scouts ahead to the elevator to make sure the coast was clear of reporters.

This bit of dramatics, however, impressed him less than did the explanations of our committee's policy and program. For later that day John Fell reappeared. Our volunteer who had first spotted him on his previous visit came hurrying back to tell me, in considerable consternation: "Not only is John Fell back, but he has his older brother Borden and three of Borden's friends with him this time!"

They were quickly escorted to our private rooms. By sheer coincidence there were no reporters or photographers in our pressroom at that moment and thus their visit went unrecorded in the press.

Borden said John Fell had told him of his earlier visit and some of the things we had explained. Borden said he would like to hear them firsthand and would like to ask some questions.

We commenced this session with a fuller explanation of the mechanics of a nominating convention. We also went into fuller detail on many of the subjects explained earlier to John Fell.

Borden, who was a student at Harvard, and his

friends, who were classmates, posed penetrating questions, mostly about the elements that create a convention trend. The session was stimulating for us, and we hoped it was for them.

Then we explained that if reporters and photographers saw Stevenson's sons at our headquarters, it might give rise to charges that we were a front organization for their father. We asked them, therefore, not to come back.

When Borden, quite disappointed, said: "You mean never come back to the Hilton Hotel?" we answered: "You can visit the Harriman, Kefauver, Russell, and Kerr headquarters as much as you like. But never come back to the fifteenth floor." We then escorted them down the back stairs to the thirteenth floor of the hotel, where another headquarters was located.[4]

[4] When they left, we gave them copies of our literature, news releases, and additional buttons. When their father came to visit us after he had been nominated, he had one of our large "America Needs Stevenson For President" buttons in his pocket. When asked where he got it, he replied: "I believe Borden and John Fell preceded me here!"

CHAPTER IV

STIMULATING INTEREST
IN THE DRAFT:
WEDNESDAY, THURSDAY, FRIDAY,
JULY 16, 17, 18

WHEN WE opened our headquarters at the Hilton on July 16, the press was full of pessimism about any possibility of the Convention's drafting Stevenson. Story after story stated that Stevenson's hope, as expressed on July 12, that all delegates would respect his desire to run for governor had ended all possibilities of a draft. The stories stressed, too, that President Truman and other party leaders, including Arvey, had given up hope for Stevenson, and many were now rallying to the candidacy of Vice-President Barkley.

A few samples from the press recapture this low point in the Stevenson draft.

The Alsops, July 17:

The movement to draft Governor Adlai Stevenson of Illinois for the Democratic nomination for President is now dead—at last for the first few ballots of the oncoming convention. As of today, in fact, Stevenson is being counted right out of the Democratic picture, even by National Committeeman Jacob Arvey of Illinois, who took the leading part until recently in the powerful draft-Stevenson drive. . . .

Marquis Childs, July 17:

. . . Gov. Adlai Stevenson has at last succeeded in eliminating himself. That, at any rate, is the verdict of the powers in the party who have been first puzzled and then angered by the Governor's determination to play the reluctant bride.

Because of this grim determination, his good friend and patron, Jacob Arvey, boss of the party in Illinois, has had his hands tied. The draft he might have engineered now seems highly improbable. Stevenson's latest statement asking the delegates not to work for him, coming minutes after Gen. Eisenhower's nomination was the final damper. . . .

Elie Abel, *New York Times*, July 16:

. . . Gov. Adlai E. Stevenson of Illinois, an early favorite of some delegates, appeared to have lost most of his supporters by his persistent refusal to declare himself an active candidate.

Robert L. Riggs reported in the *Louisville Courier-Journal* that Arvey had finally given up and "said he was going to respect the wishes of the Illinois Governor to be let alone." And Gerry Robichaud said in the *Chicago Sun-Times* on Thursday the 17th that "Arvey maintained there was little prospect that the convention would name Stevenson since the latter had made no attempt whatever to obtain the nomination."

We were faced with the blunt fact—the week be-

fore the Convention opened—that we had to counter-
act the gloom that pervaded the minds of many over
the "hopelessness of drafting Stevenson." We looked
upon ourselves as a catalytic agent to the draft, and
we contributed significantly to this by stimulating
continuously growing newspaper, radio, and TV comment about drafting Stevenson and the fact that his
name would be placed in nomination.

The mere opening of the Hilton headquarters on
July 16 started a revival of interest in the draft. Newspaper, radio, and TV reporters began to write numer-
ous stories about our committee. Soon top national
correspondents were specifically assigned to our committee. And *Life*, with our hearty co-operation, placed
Coles H. Phinizy and Bob Kelley, two photographers
—with Stevenson volunteer badges on their shirts—in
our headquarters with complete freedom to photo-
graph whatever they wished.[1]

Since we found ourselves in the unorthodox situation of not having a candidate, we adopted unorthodox
tactics to arouse interest. We issued extremely few
routine press releases extolling Stevenson. Instead,
with the aid of Stuart Haydon, we talked individually
to reporters. We emphasized that we had no connection with the Governor, and a reading of the
papers demonstrates that this fact was not questioned.

There was no doubt, we said, that the nation needed
Stevenson and so did the Democratic Party. We explained that Stevenson, a man of deep humility,
naturally questioned his qualifications for this most
difficult of posts. On the other hand, we pointed

[1] *Life*, August 4, used *one* picture!

out that he was highly qualified through his past experience to be an able, successful President.

In view of his devotion to public service—and that of his father and grandfather before him—we stated that we were convinced he could not refuse to accept an honest draft. We pointed out that this was an open Convention, there was no real leadership, and we felt that grass-roots delegates and particularly candidates for governor, senator, or congressman should take the lead in drafting Stevenson, the strongest and best candidate.[2]

As a result of our stimulation, plus the growing objections to each of the active candidates, the news about the Stevenson draft began to change quickly. By Friday, July 18, Max K. Gilstrap was saying in the *Christian Science Monitor:*

Gov. Adlai E. Stevenson didn't plan it that way—and the leading announced Democratic presidential aspirants certainly don't relish it—but the hottest conversation topic on the eve of the Democratic National Convention concerns the possibility of the Illinois Governor's being drafted.

The *Chicago Sun-Times* reported on the same day:

Despite Stevenson's refusal to seek the nomination, and Arvey's public gloom over the possibilities of drafting him, there was a resurgence of Stevenson talk during the day.

Edward T. Folliard wrote in the *Washington Post* on the 18th that the first striking aspect of the Con-

[2] See, for example, B. M. McKelway, *Washington Star,* July 23; Raymond P. Brandt, *St. Louis Post-Dispatch*, July 18; Howard Norton, *Baltimore Sun*, July 17.

vention was that this was the first "free and open" Convention in sixteen years, with the big city bosses and the White House not in control of the delegates. And he added that "secondly, there is this curious situation: the more avowed candidates arrive in Chicago, the more talk there is about a fugitive from the nomination—Gov. Adlai Stevenson of Illinois."

A major development in the movement to draft Stevenson, and one we utilized to the fullest extent possible to build favorable news coverage, centered on colorful Hoosier Governor Schricker, famed for his broad-brimmed white hat, symbol of integrity in Indiana politics.

On Monday, July 14, Schricker phoned me from Indianapolis. He had just received a telegram from us asking him to join our committee. He asked me who I was and what our committee was. I explained.

Then he said that he could not join our committee now because he did not speak for the Indiana delegation, and to join now might seem to commit Indiana's delegates.

My notes jotted down at the time reveal that he then said: "There is a statement in the Indianapolis papers that I am going to nominate Stevenson. I would be honored to do so, but no one has asked me."

I immediately asked him to place Stevenson's name in nomination. Then I explained that the convention was uncontrolled; that it was not being dictated to by Washington or by any single force. There was a great opportunity, I added, for Democratic governors and candidates for the Senate and House of Representatives to assert their leadership in the party and make it a real grass-roots-controlled party.

On this note the conversation ended. It so happened that Howard Norton of the *Baltimore Sun* was sitting in the hotel room where I took this call. Although I carefully called Schricker only "Governor" during the talk, any crack reporter would have suspected it must be Schricker in view of his long interest in drafting Stevenson.

Without mentioning Schricker, Norton headlined his story written from Chicago on the 16th: "Stevenson To Be Placed In Nomination." Such a headline bolstered the morale of pro-Stevenson delegates, who were puzzled as to who would place Stevenson's name in nomination, since Arvey and the Illinois delegation had announced that they had acceded to Stevenson's request that they not do so.

On July 17—the day Norton's headline appeared in the *Baltimore Sun*—I called Schricker. I stressed again that this was an uncontrolled Convention and told Schricker that James Reston of the *New York Times* and Robert Riggs of the *Louisville Courier-Journal,* with whom I had just talked, thought so too. I emphasized that Howard Norton in the *Baltimore Sun* had said just that this very morning.

When I added that the governors had a magnificent opportunity to take control of the Convention and nominate Stevenson, Schricker replied that many governors were not for him. I stressed then that an inner core could be formed. I asked if he would like to have a delegation call on him when he arrived in Chicago to ask him to place Stevenson's name in nomination.

My notes scribbled at the time read: "He hesitated and finally said, 'No—I will be in touch with you personally when I reach Chicago on Sunday.' "

After this call I told Reston of the *New York Times,* Norton of the *Baltimore Sun,* Raymond P. Brandt of the *St. Louis Post-Dispatch,* and one or two other reporters about the conversation. After checking, Brandt wrote on July 18 that Stevenson "is the most talked about politician in Chicago." Explaining that the Draft Committee was trying to get Schricker to lead in organizing the draft, he added: "Schricker told friends by telephone last night that he was definitely interested in helping Stevenson get the nomination but that he wanted to confer with the Illinois Governor before making a decision."

And Norton said in the *Sun* on the 18th:

. . . Governor Schricker . . . declared in a telephone talk from Indianapolis that he and the "great majority" of Indiana delegates considered Stevenson the man who would give local Democratic candidates all over the country their best chance of winning. . . .

Informed of the plan to send a committee to ask him to nominate Stevenson, Governor Schricker commented: "That may not be necessary.". . .

With favorable press stories about the Stevenson draft now beginning to appear in the nation-wide press we began on July 17 to crank out on our mimeograph machine a daily handbill quoting these stories.

"Stevenson Headlines," as they were called, were widely distributed by our volunteers. After the Con-

vention opened they were placed daily on the delegates' seats in the Convention hall. With our funds
increasing, we also prepared some by photo-offset,
including columns by Thomas L. Stokes and the
Alsops which were published on July 22.

"Stevenson Headlines" solved the problem of how
to attract the attention of the delegates and the whole
press-radio-TV corps to what was being said in the
press of the nation. "Stevenson Headlines" for July 18
is typical of those issued by us:

STEVENSON HEADLINES   Friday, July 18, 1952

*STEVENSON DRAFT GROWS AS DEM
    DEADLOCK LOOMS*

That's what the New York *Daily News* says today in a
lead article on the Democratic convention. "Talk of nominating Governor Adlai Stevenson of Illinois increased tonight as Democratic leaders conceded privately that the
wide open race among the avowed Presidential candidates
pointed to a deadlock which could be broken only by a
swing to a compromise choice," said the *News.*

"The undercurrent for a Stevenson draft grew stronger
every hour . . . Indiana's delegation, when it caucuses
Monday, may kick off the draft drive."

* * *

*GOV. SCHRICKER GIVES BOOST TO ADLAI
    BACKERS*

This was the headline in this morning's Chicago *Sun-
Times.* The newspaper said the draft-Stevenson drive was
given a lift by intimations that the Indiana Governor
might act as generalissimo of the campaign. . . . Gov.
Schricker told the *Sun-Times* "I'm very friendly toward
Gov. Stevenson and would like to be able to nominate

him." Also, the *Sun-Times* quoted the Indiana Governor as saying that Stevenson would do more than any other potential Democratic presidential nominee to "help elect Democratic candidates for state and local offices."

* * *

GOVERNORS URGED TO AID STEVENSON

The New York *Times* today reports a move was underway to persuade the Democratic governors of the nation to take the lead in drafting Gov. Stevenson for the Democratic presidential nomination. The newspaper said Gov. Henry F. Schricker of Indiana had agreed, after discussing the idea with officials of the National Committee, Stevenson for President Organization, to explore the governor's petition idea with Gov. G. Mennen Williams of Michigan and Gov. Paul A. Dever of Massachusetts.

The *Times* also quoted Col. Jacob M. Arvey, the Illinois National Committeeman, that no "patriotic American could refuse the nomination of his party at this time."

* * *

SCHRICKER EYED AS NOMINATOR

A committee of delegates was being organized to call on Gov. Schricker to put the name of Gov. Stevenson in nomination for the presidency, says the Baltimore *Sun*. Gov. Schricker told the *Sun* that he and most of Indiana's 30 delegates would vote for Stevenson if they got a chance.

* * *

While we avoided issuing too many routine press releases, we did issue several unorthodox items— "background pieces"—which, with their sharp variation from the usual press handout, delighted newsmen. The "background piece" we issued on Friday, July 18 —prepared by Ralph Newman of the Abraham Lin-

coln Bookstore of Chicago—attracted the most attention. Entitled "It Happened in Chicago in 1880," this
piece was designed to help convince uncommitted
delegates that a man who didn't want the nomination, and who had opposed having his name placed
in nomination, had actually received the nomination
once before. This release, too, furnished useful information for our volunteers in persuading delegates,
hesitant to commit themselves, that a draft was possible since it had happened before.

The release read:

The Honorable Adlai E. Stevenson, Governor of Illinois
whose name is high on the list of probable candidates for
the Democratic Presidential nomination stands an excellent chance of seeing history repeat itself in Chicago!

Just 72 years ago, prior to Convention time, the name
of James A. Garfield, of Ohio, was mentioned as a likely
presidential candidate. Garfield's comments on the situation sound, as we review them, almost identical to the
Stevenson utterances of the past few months. Garfield
said, "While I am not indifferent to the good opinion of
men who think me fit for that high place, I am still wholly
disinclined to believe that any good will come of it." And,
"I have long and so often seen the evil effects of the presidential fever upon my associates and friends that I am
determined it shall not seize upon me, for in almost every
case it impairs if it does not destroy the usefulness of its
victim." The well-known biographer of Garfield, Theodore C. Smith, speaks of Garfield's attitude toward the
nomination: "All evidence in existence shows that Garfield was not even a receptive candidate, but tended to
view the 'dark horse' movement with disquiet if not actual alarm . . . he did not want it [the presidency] and

was not a candidate for it, but could not absolutely say in advance that he would not take it, since it was conceivable that his party might really need him."

Garfield came to Chicago to manage the campaign of his friend, Senator John Sherman of Ohio. The other candidates were General Grant (for a third term), Senator James G. Blaine of Maine, and Senator George F. Edmunds of Vermont. Senator George F. Hoar of Massachusetts was permanent chairman of the convention. Garfield delivered the Sherman nomination speech and captivated the delegates and the spectators. He received an ovation lasting twenty-five minutes. On the first ballot Grant received 304 votes, Blaine 284, Sherman 93, Edmunds 33, with some scattered votes for a few favorite sons. Then followed a long-drawn-out struggle through 33 ballots. On the 34th ballot Garfield received 17 votes and at once arose and voiced a question of order. He said, "I challenge the correctness of the announcement. No man has a right, without the consent of the person voted for, to announce that person's name, and vote for him in this Convention. Such consent I have not given. . . ." At this point Chairman Hoar interrupted Garfield and ruled him out of order. The roll call was resumed and on the 35th ballot Garfield received 50 votes. The 36th ballot was then taken and Garfield received 399 votes and was nominated.

Garfield sat motionless. He seemed stunned by surprise. He almost collapsed and was taken out of the Convention Hall and moved to a hotel. He had sincerely tried to avoid the nomination, even to the point of objecting while the actual balloting was being carried on, yet he was his party's choice and was carried to victory in November over the Democratic nominee, Winfield S. Hancock.

The reluctant candidate can be successful!

Zachary Taylor wrote several letters disavowing his interest in the Presidency, yet he was elected in 1848.

In 1859 Abraham Lincoln wrote to T. J. Pickett and said: "I must in candor say I do not think myself fit for the Presidency."

In 1844 James K. Polk received the Democratic nomination on the 9th ballot. He was not voted on at all until the 8th ballot, and he was his party's first "dark horse" candidate.

Franklin Pierce's name did not appear before the Convention in 1852 until the 29th ballot. He was the party's choice on the 49th ballot!

Martin Van Buren, 8th President of the United States, was one of the most practical politicians who ever occupied the White House. In a letter to his son, written in 1858, he said: "the people will never make a man President who is so importunate as to show by his life and conversation that he not only has his eye upon, but is in active pursuit of, the office. . . . This they reserve as a free-will offering. Some men have reached it by accident . . . but no man who laid himself out for it and was unwise enough to let people into his secret, ever yet obtained it." Van Buren, the "Little Magician," was right and Henry Clay, Daniel Webster, William Jennings Bryan and Robert A. Taft, among other disappointed aspirants, can certainly attest to the wisdom of his comments.

Clearly history is on the side of Adlai E. Stevenson of Illinois! She is eager to repeat—and in Chicago—after 72 years!

The release attracted considerable attention and was one more item creating publicity for the Stevenson draft. Bob Considine in the Hearst press for July 21, for instance, summarized it and then wrote: "The Stevenson-For-President people die hard, and not without scholarship. Their yearning for their man to change his mind resulted in a communique from Gov. Stevenson's unauthorized headquarters which could have been the work of John Kieran. Most such ultimatums are dreary dross. But not this."

Friday the 18th, the day we issued "It Happened in Chicago in 1880," Stevenson arrived in Chicago from Springfield, where he had been secluded from the press for some days. Met at the airport by a barrage of reporters and TV and newsreel cameras, he said:

"I shall never be a candidate in the sense that I'll ask anybody to vote for me here. On the contrary, I'll do everything possible to discourage any delegate from putting me in nomination or nominating me.

"I cannot conceive that, with all the willing candidates available and with all the talent and ability at its disposal, the Democratic party would turn to an unwilling candidate who is running for another office."

When told that Schricker or Archibald Alexander of New Jersey might place his name in nomination, Stevenson replied that he would do everything he possibly could to discourage them.

In reporting this incident for the *New York Times*, James Reston observed:

Gov. Adlai E. Stevenson of Illinois arrived in Chicago today and immediately took one more long step toward eliminating himself from the Democratic Presidential nomination.

. . . This was further than the Governor had ever gone

in his attempt to discourage his nomination, but he repeated previous statements that if the convention drafted him against his wishes he would decide what to do at that time.

Realizing that Stevenson's statement might dampen the draft, which by now was beginning to gain momentum, we released this statement over my name:

Governor Stevenson, by his statement at the airport several hours ago, has created a situation which will put the Convention delegates and alternates to the supreme task of nominating without any encouragement the strongest and most popular candidate for the Presidency. Our minds have not been changed that Governor Stevenson must and will accept a draft.

I am of the firm conviction Governor Stevenson never would dictate to the delegates in any way which would prevent them from exercising their free right to select the man they think is best qualified to be President.

CHAPTER V

THE DELEGATES COME TO SEE US: WEDNESDAY, THURSDAY, FRIDAY, JULY 16, 17, 18

"SCORES OF delegates took the unprecedented step of going, quite spontaneously, to offer their support to the amateur draft-Stevenson headquarters," the Alsops wrote on July 24. Actually, from July 16 to July 18 about three hundred delegates visited our headquarters.

The *Chicago Daily News* (July 17) in an editorial expressed the belief that delegates might view our headquarters "as a fake arranged by a sly and ambitious candidate" and that this might "irritate the delegates to a point of complete loss of interest." This never occurred. The delegates, as far as we knew, and the news reports about our Draft Committee accepted us for what we were—an unofficial draft movement.

We helped crystallize the draft by having headquarters where delegates favoring Stevenson could receive information about Stevenson supporters in other delegations. If we had not been in existence in these days just prior to the opening of the Convention, many of these delegates might have lost confidence and committed themselves to support someone else. We helped keep firm their faith that Stevenson could and would be drafted.

The delegates were interviewed by our more experienced volunteers. These included the executive committee and a few others who were lawyers, teachers, and businessmen in their thirties and forties. Our volunteers who greeted visitors at the elevators were students, teachers, and housewives, many of them in their twenties.

As some of our visitors were ardent supporters of Kefauver, Harriman, or Russell, these volunteers in the hotel foyer were instructed not to argue with them. They were advised instead to say: "I prefer Stevenson; you are entitled to your view. But if you would like more information about Stevenson, we will arrange an interview with our delegate-contact people." We hoped by this approach to avoid the bitterness that had developed at the Republican Convention between the Eisenhower and Taft supporters. We were also most anxious that the supporters of the various candidates be kept in a friendly mood so they could rally behind Stevenson when the proper moment came.

Our system of having the volunteers at the elevators channel delegates and newsmen to the correct rooms did not always work smoothly. Some of the volunteers did not always recognize national figures. One day, for instance, Solicitor General Philip B. Perlman was kept waiting in the foyer of the fifteenth floor for twenty minutes.

Many leading Democrats visited our headquarters in the first days, from July 16 to 18. Jonathan Daniels, White House assistant to both Franklin D. Roosevelt and Harry S. Truman, and editor of the *Raleigh News*

and Observer, and Mrs. Charles Tillett of North Carolina, formerly Vice-Chairman of the Democratic National Committee, were among those who came and
were helpful with advice and support. Mrs. Tillett
brought a number of delegates to our headquarters to
meet with us. She was present one day when a leading
figure in the Ohio delegation came in to see Hubert
Will.

The Ohioan asked: "Where is Stevenson's campaign manager?"

Will replied: "Stevenson is not a candidate. There
isn't any campagin manager. We have co-chairmen
and volunteers to interview delegates."

The Ohio leader said: "Well, let me talk to Stevenson."

Will replied: "Don't you know that this is a headquarters without a candidate?"

The Ohioan then said: "Well, with whom do I
deal?"

Will replied: "We can't deal except that maybe
we can give you a seconding speech to make."

"Oh!" said the Ohioan, a bit surprised. "Well, keep
in touch with me on the floor of the convention."
(We did. He voted for Senator Russell for two ballots and switched to Stevenson on the third.)

When he had left, Mrs. Tillett remarked: "He never
met a situation like this before in his political experience. This is the most inspiring convention I've ever
attended. It's wonderful for the country and the
Democratic Party that delegates are free to choose the
best man."

Among the other visitors in these opening days

were Frank E. Karelsen, Jr., experienced convention-goer and former treasurer of the New York Democratic Party; Kenneth Anderson, National Committeeman elect, and John Young, state chairman, both of Kansas; Dwight Palmer and Mrs. Thorn Lord of New Jersey; and, on Saturday morning the 19th, James A. Finnegan, president of the Philadelphia City Council, and Francis J. Myers, former Senator from Pennsylvania.

When Myers and Finnegan discovered that our tabulation of votes for Stevenson in the Pennsylvania delegation was the same as theirs, Myers said: "We're glad to see you fellows here."

Many of the delegates were for Stevenson at this early point, but they were disturbed over two questions. They didn't want to know about Stevenson's record—they knew what this was and were for him. But they wanted to know whether he would accept if nominated. And, second, they wanted to know if his name would be placed in nomination.

These delegates for Stevenson needed no convincing by our committee that the Governor was the one candidate—other than Vice-President Barkley—who could appeal to the many factions in the party. They obviously wanted a middle-of-the-road man to lead their party. They also needed no convincing of his vote-getting abilities. They knew of his 572,000 margin of victory for Governor in 1948.

These delegates wanted to win the election, and they felt that Stevenson was the most formidable man they had. Newspaper reports seemed to substantiate this belief in their own minds. Walter Lippmann noted: "Gov. Stevenson's position is unique in that he alone is not certain to alienate any of the main factions of the party." And Clifton Utley wrote: "Adlai Stevenson is a brilliant campaigner, a proven vote-getter, and in nearly every way an answer to the campaign manager's prayer. . . . To the extent that any person is in a position to accomplish two irreconcilable things at once, Stevenson should be able to hold the South while attracting minority groups and other blocs of votes the Democrats need to win in the North." [1]

Many of the delegates relished the idea of supporting a man who was not "a cut and dried candidate selected by party bosses." As Thomas L. Stokes pointed out (July 22): "The delegates could stand up on their own feet, free and fearless Americans. . . . Stevenson offered the excitement of the hunt. The more he shied away, the more attractive he became. Well, they'd just bag him for themselves, on their own, and no longer could any flip newspaper reporters describe them as a lost mob waiting for 'the word.' "

But they wanted to know from us: would he accept if nominated? These delegates did not want to look foolish by supporting a man who would reject a nomination. They remembered vividly that certain party leaders had come out for General Dwight Eisenhower as the Democratic candidate in 1948, only to be left "naked as jay-birds when Eisenhower refused to run" (the Alsops, July 17).

[1] See the *Chicago Sun-Times*, July 18, for both columns. David Lawrence wrote on July 21: "It would be a feather in Stevenson's cap to get the nomination unsolicited, as he would not be obligated to any faction in the party. He would be a serious contender against Gen. Eisenhower."

We explained to the delegates that we could not conceive how a man as dedicated to public service as Stevenson could reject an honest draft. And whenever delegates quoted his statements that he didn't want to be nominated, we agreed that he didn't, but added that he had never made a statement like General Sherman's, that he would not run if nominated.

Hubert Will in talking to delegates explained that he had seen Stevenson on April 14. On that occasion Stevenson had read the statement he issued on April 16 that he could only be a candidate for governor. Will had failed to dissuade him from issuing the statement. The conversation had broken up with Will's saying that he didn't see how a man of principle like Stevenson could refuse a call to a higher public service. Will added that the Draft Committee would continue its activity, based on this belief, unless the Governor announced that he would not accept if nominated.

The real question to those of us of the Draft Committee was not: Would he accept if nominated? Knowing the quality of his mind—*and he never told us he would accept if nominated*—we could not conceive how he could refuse. The real question in our minds, therefore, was: Would the Convention nominate Stevenson in spite of his clear, firm position that he was not a candidate?

The question whether his name would be placed in nomination caused us some difficulty the first day we opened at the Hilton Hotel. We decided that day on our own that his name must be placed in nomination on the first ballot. We reached this decision after talking to a number of delegates, who made it clear they feared that unless his name was placed in nomination on the first ballot, the draft might disintegrate.

We now had to find a delegate of prominence who would nominate him. Fortunately, the next day—Thursday, the 17th—we found such a delegate. Archibald Alexander, former Under Secretary of the Army and then campaigning in New Jersey for the Senate seat held by H. Alexander Smith, came to our headquarters, introduced himself, and told us that if no better-known leader would place Stevenson's name in nomination, he would.

Alexander's statement to us required courage. We were an unofficial group with no recognition from most party leaders. President Truman and the inner leaders of the party, according to the current news stories, had given up the idea of the draft and many of them now were forming behind the candidacy of Vice-President Barkley.[2] Alexander, however, like many others in the party wanted dynamic, youthful

[2] See, for instance, the Alsops' column for July 24 reviewing this situation. Governor Dever of Massachusetts said on July 20 that it was his view that Stevenson was not available for the nomination (*New York Times,* July 21). Archibald Alexander wrote me on March 23, 1954: ". . . you might wish to stress a little more the great difficulty encountered in trying to interest the professionals in the Stevenson candidacy during the early and late spring of 1952. At least my own experience . . . indicates that in Pennsylvania, Massachusetts, Ohio and Illinois (in the last of these no doubt because of the request of Governor Stevenson to Colonel Arvey) I found it impossible to get any agreement to try to band together and to form a strong nucleus working in advance of and during the convention for the nomination of Governor Stevenson. You will remember that I met with expressions of admiration for him, but also the ever-present fear of backing a loser, or even more embarrassing, a candidate who wouldn't run."

leadership. An old personal friend of Stevenson's, he worked vigorously to put the draft over.

Stevenson had encouraged Alexander to campaign for the Senate in a conversation in March 1952, on the ground that the Democratic Party needed younger people of integrity and training in elective as well as appointive office.

Before coming to Chicago, Alexander had discussed the Stevenson candidacy with Mayor David Lawrence of Pittsburgh, Michael DiSalle of Ohio, and Governor Paul Dever of Massachusetts. Dever made it clear to Alexander that he was not prepared to come out for or work for Stevenson unless Stevenson was a candidate. Lawrence and DiSalle, both of whom preferred Stevenson, felt the chances that the Convention would nominate him were slim. In spite of these discouraging talks, Alexander continued to work for the Stevenson nomination.

Early in July he had phoned Stevenson in Springfield. Stevenson reiterated that he wished to run for governor. Stevenson told Alexander that he was being so hard-pressed by the demand he run for President that he might find it necessary to state he would not do so even if nominated. This Alexander urged him not to do, for the good of the entire party.

When Stevenson arrived in Chicago on Friday, July 18, and told reporters he hoped Alexander would not place his name in nomination, we were faced with a major crisis in our plans. Governor Schricker had not yet agreed to place Stevenson's name in nomination. If Alexander was called off, the draft might collapse. Alexander was in touch with us at once. We pointed out that we might have to abandon our efforts if he changed his mind about placing Stevenson's name in nomination. Alexander assured us that, although Stevenson's statement had made it difficult for him, he was prepared to abide by his position.[3]

From the standpoint of launching the draft at the Convention, Alexander's statement on July 17 was vital. Now the delegates could be told that Stevenson's name would be placed in nomination. The delegates naturally were loath to go all out for a draft that gave them no assurance that Stevenson's name would even be placed in nomination.

Alexander has said that after the newspapers carried the story that he was available to place Stevenson's name in nomination, "I must have heard from delegates of approximately twenty different states who seemed to have no place else to turn to and who indicated their interest in Stevenson." [4]

Even after Alexander's pledge, some leaders tried to persuade us not to place Stevenson's name in nomination, but let his name attract a few votes without a formal nomination. Then, when a deadlock occurred, a dramatic shift to Stevenson could be made.

It was clear that advocates of this strategy had in mind the draft of James Garfield. But a draft, to be a legitimate one, didn't have to wait until a deadlock. Charles Evans Hughes had been placed in nomination

[3] Alexander has written that "it is of course clear that Stevenson himself did everything he could to discourage those who sought to nominate him."

[4] On September 2, 1952 Alexander prepared a short memorandum on how Stevenson was drafted.

in 1916 before the first ballot when he was not a candidate. And he received the nomination on the third
ballot.[5]

Our committee, beginning on July 17, was able
to stress that we knew Stevenson would be placed in
nomination on the first ballot. We felt this step was
just as legitimate a draft as waiting for a deadlock.
Moreover, the historical proclivity of the Democrats
to row over the nominee for ballot after ballot—44 in
1912, and 103 in 1924—made waiting for a deadlock
too risky and stupid.

On Friday afternoon, July 18, we issued this press
release:

The turn of events since last night toward the draft of
Governor Stevenson has unquestionably developed the
existence of a key group of strong Stevenson supporters
in the convention. This answers the necessity of being
able to advise those delegations who wish to join the draft
that they have, in fact, a voting nucleus around which
they can rally.

The National Committee for Stevenson is now convinced that Governor Stevenson's name will go into nomi-

[5] See Merlo J. Pusey: *Charles Evans Hughes* (New York: Mac-
millan Co.; 1951), Vol. I, pp. 326–8. Stevenson apparently felt like
Hughes, who said after the second ballot: "if they will only choose
some one else at Chicago today and let me go out West with my
family this summer, I'll be the happiest man in the world." There
were other similarities between 1916 and 1952. Pusey points out that
the only real groundswell at the Convention centered on Hughes.
Hughes had no headquarters, no representatives, no badges, no literature. Pusey writes: "Frank Hitchcock, whose work for Hughes had
earned only repudiation, kept repeating that Hughes would be nominated on the third ballot. 'Nobody seemed to be for Hughes,' he
said, 'except the people.' "

nation during the nominating roll-call. This knowledge we have from several who have offered to do so.[6] It will be their decision how and by whom this will be done. Many delegates have been in conference with us during the last few hours. Their prime concern is information about the feeling of other delegations. This we have supplied.

It looks to us that the heart of the Stevenson movement comes from the Democratic party around the country, but particularly from some governors and candidates for the Senate and House of Representatives who know that Governor Stevenson will be a great asset to their own campaigns. This is healthy. This would indicate, above all else, that this is an uncontrolled convention.

This press release with the blunt statement that Stevenson's name would be placed in nomination on the roll-call was highly significant to the draft movement. It was the first public statement of positive Convention action. Up to this time our efforts had been to stimulate talk about the draft. Now the delegates had the concrete information that the draft had formalized to the extent that Stevenson would be placed in nomination.

The release also encouraged many delegates to pay us their first visit when they realized that the draft was now more than the wild dream of an unofficial committee.

[6] By this time William Carlebach of New York, Sanford Petersky of Washington, and Frank Hutton of North Carolina had told us that in case no nationally known figure could be secured to nominate Stevenson, they would do it.

CHAPTER VI

PENNSYLVANIA HOLDS THE KEY:
SATURDAY, JULY 19

OUR DRAFT COMMITTEE had assumed, when we opened headquarters on July 16, that all we had to do was to serve as a clearing-house of information for delegates and as a center for the stimulation of news about Stevenson. But we soon discovered the truth of what Dewey Fleming wrote in the *Baltimore Sun* on Friday, the 18th: "Chicago is filling up with a throng of leaderless and bewildered delegates and minor local bosslets looking vainly for someone to tell them which way to go and what to do."

By Saturday, the 19th, we knew that we would have to aid the delegates plan the organization of the draft. The delegates had to be organized, a floor leader selected, and someone chosen to place Stevenson's name in nomination.

That Saturday afternoon Kenneth Anderson, National Committeeman from Kansas, called a meeting at his headquarters in the Palmer House to discuss the Stevenson draft. For an hour there were conflicting views presented as to what should be done. Walter Reuther's C.I.O. representative coyly refused to commit himself at all and said he was present merely as an observer. Governor Oren E. Long of Hawaii said his delegation planned to vote for Truman on the first ballot because the President had been such a strong supporter of statehood, but after that they were not sure. Francis Biddle, former Attorney General and a delegate from the District of Columbia, said there was a strong Stevenson current among delegates, but wondered whether it might be best *not* to place his name in nomination on the first ballot.

Anderson, however, described how strongly Kansas was for Stevenson, and Archibald Alexander did the same for New Jersey. Representatives from Pennsylvania and Indiana also pointed to the strong Stevenson sentiment in their delegations.

At this point we reported that a conservative estimate based on our delegate files revealed that Stevenson would receive a minimum of 75 votes on the first ballot. This figure did not include what he might receive from the Illinois delegation. On the second ballot we expected between 60 and 100 additional votes.

Near the end of the meeting there was a discussion of crystallizing the drafting procedure, but the meeting broke up with no firm plans having been made.

About thirty minutes after this meeting, Lewis M. Stevens, Philadelphia City Council member and an old Princeton friend of Stevenson, called at our headquarters to talk to me. An hour after this visit, Stevens phoned me. He told me that James Finnegan, President of the Philadelphia City Council, and he had been discussing the results of their earlier visits to our headquarters. Stevens said they would like to talk to me as soon as possible.

At this critical point in the draft movement the

unsuccessful Kansas meeting had dramatized to us the
need of developing a solid core of delegates working
toward a definite nominating schedule. With this in
mind, I suggested an immediate meeting with Stevens
and Finnegan in their headquarters.

I think a brief word on the general circumstances of
the pre-Convention "climate" might be in order. From
noon on, this Saturday the 19th, paraders, hecklers,
bands, drum teams, and all the sideshow elements of a
traditional orthodox convention filled the hotels and
streets of Chicago's Loop district.

We had none of these.

But our fifteenth floor was swarming with hundreds
of Stevenson volunteers, delegates, and alternate delegates. They were the real working parts of the Convention, not the hoopla and noise of the hotel lobbies
and streets.

The weather was hot—oppressive. The climate of
the nomination contest was hot—and, to some, de-
pressive.

Here it was, almost up to the deadline—the opening of the Convention formalities. In a sense, we had
done our job—we had helped keep alive Stevenson's
name, the knowledge of his ability, and the wisdom of
his choice. None of our committee were delegates, but
we had infused our beliefs and enthusiasm into many
who were. What now?

We had one unfilled obligation: to ensure that
Stevenson's name would be put in nomination under
circumstances and conditions that would reflect the
growing popular support for him.

First off, we had decided to have no demonstrations,

no banners, bands, or banquets. Our alternative was dignity and serious concern for the importance of the destiny that was in the hands of the Convention delegates.

In our minds, the matter of a convention of delegates choosing a man who might be our next President was more weighty and more serious than bowing to expediency and "muscle-bound" political patterns. We felt these, too, were the characteristics of Stevenson.

We realized above all else that we had been, were, and would be talking about Stevenson; not for him. This was a position unique in the politics of a national convention.

As it developed, this proved to be our strongest point of argument. With some of the delegates, of course, it took considerable discussion to explain that we did not and could not speak for Stevenson. Once past this hurdle, occasionally made difficult by some of the innuendoes that we were a "front" for this or that group, we got into the wisdom of nominating Stevenson.

The opportunity came on this hot, hectic 19th day of July to put all this planning, logic, and enthusiasm to a crucial test in this meeting with leaders of the Pennsylvania delegation.

Here was a delegation from a leading industrial state with the voting strength, know-how, and personalities that could carry the assignment of political action. We felt perfectly justified in offering to outline the opportunity we saw. As I have written, Finnegan and Myers had visited our headquarters that morning. They had seen the files that Ming, Will, and Holleb had on the Convention delegates. They had been given a breakdown of our knowledge of the situation within their delegation. It was accurate. And who was better to evaluate that estimate than the leaders of the delegation?

Stuart Haydon and I met with Stevens, Finnegan, and William Teefy, another member of the delegation, at their Morrison Hotel headquarters. Their rooms were air-conditioned and therefore a comfortable relief from what we had just left at the Hilton.

On our way over, we assumed that these experienced people had canvassed the situation thoroughly.[1] We reasoned that while the trend and feeling toward Stevenson were stronger than for the candidates in the field, his nomination, nevertheless, was possible only after the organizing and planning of the actual draft—that without these the mechanics of a convention nomination was impossible. So we met.

We were asked first if our estimate of growing Stevenson strength had any serious flaws in it. We replied that if there were any faulty calculations, they

[1] We had been told by a Philadelphia reporter on the 15th that Finnegan had said he didn't care what Stevenson said or Arvey said, he was coming to Chicago to fight for Stevenson. We later learned that Myers, who had arrived in Chicago on July 15 to work on the platform committee, had been in touch by phone with Finnegan every day. Myers reported that Frank McKinney, Chairman of the National Committee, and other leaders all said Vice-President Barkley was the man to be nominated. Finnegan in Philadelphia replied: "Nothing doing. It must be Stevenson." At a meeting of some Pennsylvania delegates in Harrisburg on June 9 to hear Estes Kefauver, Finnegan had said: "This is purely a courtesy visit. My presence here does not mean that I am backing the Senator. In my mind, I believe the national convention is going to draft Governor Stevenson" (*Philadelphia Bulletin*, June 9).

were on the conservative side—the result of our precaution in back-checking on commitments made by delegates.

We then said we would like to give them our evaluation of the position of Pennsylvania and the realities of the Convention as we saw them. (They told us later that this action of complete frankness and bluntness was a governing factor in their subsequent decision to work with us.)

This is what we said:

"We realize that there are some cold, hard political factors in this situation. We do not speak for Adlai Stevenson. We can only speak about him. This means that anyone who gets up on the floor and places him in nomination, any group which undertakes floor leadership in behalf of his nomination, will have no political tools with which to work. No promises can be made. There are no compromises on issues that can be made and there is no assurance even that if nominated any of us would be called in for election-campaign action.

"We realize that, fundamentally, working toward the nomination of Adlai Stevenson will have one concrete reward: the personal satisfaction that a dignified, competent, and honorable man has been offered as the Democratic Party's choice for the highest post in the land. That in essence is the fundamental philosophy which made the nation great. The tide is now turning from the domination of conventions by cliques of leaders back to the strength of free majority decisions.

"We are unable to give you any assurance that the evaluation we have made of the votes which will go to

Stevenson will hold the test of political fire. That is, we have no assurance other than that they have been expressed to us with the same sincerity with which we believe in the man. We have no political coercive force to hold them.

"We feel that the convention is 'uncontrolled' in the sense that no single standing candidate nor any bloc of candidates can reach a compromise or alter their course to a successful 'agreement.' "

These observations were then discussed more in detail in terms of the standing situation on the North-South-FEPC issues. We agreed that the extreme Northern liberals and most of the conservative Southern elements could never come to an agreement on these issues satisfactory to one another and still retain the support of their own delegates.

Finnegan made it clear that he felt a too parochial viewpoint was influencing too many delegates. Instead of taking a broad national view of the situation, he said, they were much too interested in the situation in their own states to the detriment of the broader welfare.

We then continued: "We suggest we can only offer our opinions, and that you and your delegation must decide if they make sense. Should you decide they do, then we will undertake as our final obligation to set about organizing the nominating machinery with you.

"Now, we have outlined to you, as frankly as we know how, why we feel Adlai Stevenson can be nominated, why we feel he should be, and why the next step belongs to actual delegates. There remains the major factor of 'Will he accept?' "

At this point Finnegan made this observation and asked the deciding question: Assume that there is truth in all that you say. Assume further that the Pennsylvania delegation gives a majority of its votes to Stevenson on the first ballot and that we announce that decision following a caucus. Assume, too, that other delegations do likewise and that all this might lead to a nomination after two or three ballots. How do we know he will accept it? Many people have tried to get him to commit himself, even privately—and he has refused to do so.[2] What can you say that indicates he will accept the nomination?

We replied: "For a political leader to stick his neck out in support of Stevenson without assurance of his acceptance can well be the greatest political gamble of the century. We feel and have been acting on the premise that he will not refuse.

"We reason this way: Adlai Stevenson knows that no matter how much he, or any other person, may desire to be President of the United States, it first must be the will of a convention assembled to nominate him. Therefore, if he is chosen by the same Conven-

[2] Mayor Lawrence of Pittsburgh, National Committeeman from Pennsylvania, wrote me on April 15, 1954: ". . . When I arrived in Chicago, which I think was the Thursday before the Convention opened, to serve on the Credentials Committee of the National Committee, I found, as you know, a chaotic condition relative to the situation, particularly as to Stevenson's desires, and we could not get, as you know, any definite expression that he would accept.

". . . From the time we arrived in Chicago, we constantly pressed to get some indication either on the record or off the record from Governor Stevenson, as to whether or not he would look favorably upon receiving the nomination. As you know, we drew a 'blank.' "

tion assembled, under the process which he recognizes to be the tradition of our nation, he has no right in good conscience to refuse. We believe him to be a man of good conscience, who therefore will not refuse.

"Furthermore, believing him to be a man of good conscience, we know that if the Convention were to choose him, as has been forecast far enough in the past, he has command of language excellent enough to have said long ago he would not accept—this to forestall any embarrassment to anyone who may honestly and conscientiously work for his nomination. It is not in the nature of his integrity to permit such a thing to occur."

We added: "We feel that Stevenson believes that the process of choosing a candidate should be really the choice of the delegates. He seems to reflect what so many individual citizens feel: that the Democratic Party must come to a decision in this Convention premised on current requirements—today's conditions supported by all the sound traditions of the past. That these sound traditions have been scuttled is the fear of many. That the procedure of disproving this fear is to allow the forces of free choice to prevail. Mind you, these are suppositions on our part, based only on our own evaluations and interpretations of his record."

Directly to Finnegan's question we said: "Accepting your assumptions up to the point of your question leaves us with this question. In lieu of a written statement from Adlai Stevenson to the effect he will accept the nomination, you have nothing on which to base a decision except belief in the man. Would a written commitment make him any greater? Would a written commitment endow him with any greater ability, any deeper integrity, any more acceptable personality?

"There are thousands of people across the country— not delegates, not political leaders—who have found ways to express their understanding of the emotions and feelings which go into the make-up of Adlai Stevenson's actions—or lack of them, whichever you wish. These are the people who ultimately must be satisfied.

"The reversal of the American ideal of the 'office seeking the man,' which has marked our recent political history, seems to be at an end. If the democratic process is to survive, someone along the line must pull up and take a good look at what has happened to our political procedures.

"We realize this sounds exceedingly idealistic. We admit that it is. But we will not admit that it is completely outside the bounds of political realism. We point to you what has been accomplished thus far this past week. Without funds, without traditional political organization, without even being delegates —our group has helped bring it about that Adlai Stevenson is the most serious contender for the nomination."

When we finished, there were a few moments of silence. Then we were asked how many of the large "America Needs Stevenson" buttons we had left. We replied that we thought they had all been distributed. Could we get more made in a few hours? We didn't know, but would find out. How much were they? That, neither of us could answer exactly because the design and purchase had been handled by several others in our group.

We were then told that all we had said would be taken up at the Pennsylvania caucus the next day and that they would get in touch with us just as soon as they had reached a decision.

Then for a few minutes general conversation centered on how and why we had done certain things and issued certain releases during the past week. Each time we explained our planned operations and they acknowledged that these had worked.

Just as we were about to leave, we were asked if we could accept a check so that we could have more Stevenson buttons made.

Could we? Of course we could and did.

We told them that we would try to find enough buttons, on or off our volunteers, to supply at least the Pennsylvania delegation if they wanted to emerge from their caucus wearing them.

A simple reply to our good-humored offer summed up the key results of our meeting. Finnegan said: "That's what we mean."

He then made it clear that some of them were willing to take the gamble of advocating Stevenson at their caucus. Willing to take the risk, he added, to get the best candidate for the nation.

On the way back to the Hilton, we reasoned that here was the nucleus for the whole final stage of the draft movement. These people of the Pennsylvania delegation were not naïve in the ways of political conventions. Nor were they without a record of themselves having achieved a crusade; they had uprooted a long-entrenched corrupt Republican regime in Philadelphia. They had also spearheaded a city charter that tossed out patronage, heretofore the lifeblood of a political machine.

That was not unlike the current situation. There were no political promises, no patronage plums, no assignments with kudos, as a reward or as an inducement to support the Stevenson draft. We concluded that this had been the crucial test—that these Philadelphia leaders had decided during this meeting to work closely with our committee.

Certainly what we had just experienced was so far removed from what is regarded as traditional smoke-filled-room procedure that it was almost unbelievable.

When we arrived back at the Hilton, rumors of "shifts" and "deals" going on in many headquarters, and factions, necessitated sifting them for substantiation or rejection. There was nothing to be done regarding the Pennsylvania delegation until it had come to a decision at its caucus.

We did, however, set about gathering together seventy buttons to send to them. Some had to be removed from the shirts of our volunteers to reach that high figure.

We reasoned that the Pennsylvania caucus, one of the first to be held, would be heavily covered by press, radio, and perhaps television. It was. The impact of some of the delegation emerging from the caucus wearing Stevenson buttons would be greater than if we had announced having had a satisfactory meeting before the caucus. Even though our group might have gained a little publicity at the time, it would not have been of the same value as the impact of an action taken by a delegation. Nor was it in our province to imply that this delegation was going to work with us.

CHAPTER VII

THE DRAFT FINDS A FLOOR LEADER: SUNDAY, JULY 20

SUNDAY, THE 20th, was hot, hectic, and critical.

That morning a group of leaders in the Pennsylvania delegation held a meeting in the Blackstone Hotel suite of James P. Clark, former chairman of the Philadelphia Democratic Committee. Those present were David Lawrence, Francis J. Myers, State Senator Joseph Barr, Michael Lawler, chairman of Lackawanna County, James Finnegan, Genevieve Blatt, secretary of the Democratic State Committee, and William Teefy.

They decided to urge their caucus that coming evening to endorse candidates. They were confident that the good vote Stevenson would receive would encourage other delegations to reveal their Stevenson strength.

Meanwhile Stevenson attended services at the Fourth Presbyterian Church, where the Reverend Harrison Ray Anderson preached on the text: "If any of you lack wisdom, let him ask of God, that giveth to all men liberally, and upbraideth not; and it shall be given him." The many reporters present interpreted the sermon as being directed at Stevenson, who was a personal friend of the minister. And they emphasized that Dr. Anderson seemed to be admonishing him not to decline to run if nominated. When they asked Stevenson what he thought of the sermon, he replied: "Superb."

Later that hot Sunday afternoon Stevenson met with the Illinois delegation. Reporters were barred from the caucus, but they stretched out on the floor of the anteroom. By putting their ears to the bottom of a sliding partition, they heard the give-and-take. Stevenson stated that he did not want to be nominated; that he wanted to do what he had undertaken to do and what Illinois Democrats had nominated him to do—run for re-election as Governor. "I do not dream myself fit for the job—temperamentally, mentally, or physically," the reporters heard him say. "And I ask therefore that you all abide by my wishes not to nominate me, nor to vote for me if I should be nominated."

When he concluded, Arvey was reported to have said that he would respect Stevenson's request that Illinois not nominate him. But should his name be placed in nomination, Arvey said:

When that happens I consider I am relieved from any promise I have made not to further his candidacy. He cannot take away from me my right to cast my ballot as I wish to cast it. If I am convinced that a vote for Stevenson is a vote to unify the party and win the election in November, I will vote for him.

When the caucus broke up, reporters asked Stevenson whether he would yield to a draft in the event of a Convention deadlock. "Show me the deadlock first," he replied.

Our Draft Committee then issued this statement over my name:

The meeting of the Illinois caucus a few hours ago was the last opportunity Governor Stevenson had to announce he would not accept a draft.

He did not say, nor imply, that he would refuse the call of the convention to lead the Democratic Party this fall.

I have always believed that Governor Stevenson, in view of his distinguished record of public service, would not reject a genuine desire on the part of the nation to ask him to continue such service at a higher level.

Our release led Paul Ringler to say in the *Milwaukee Journal* on July 21:

One of the paradoxical things in this picture is that the Committee's major job since it moved into the Hilton last week has been to contradict the man who is its candidate, but isn't.

Gov. Stevenson will say: "I want no part of this business" and the Committee will rush out a statement that says in effect: "Pay no attention to this man."

About nine o'clock that evening we decided to call a meeting at our headquarters for eleven p.m. We felt that the time had now come to formalize the draft procedure. We sent members of our group to find the leaders from New Jersey, Indiana, Pennsylvania, and Kansas. These were the states where the largest organized Stevenson support existed. And these states had the leadership and the experience to guide the draft on the Convention floor.

Attending the meeting at eleven that night were Finnegan and Myers of Philadelphia; Lawrence of

Pittsburgh; Schricker, Paul M. Butler (National Committeeman elect), Congressman Winfield K. Denton, Howard Whitecotton, and Frank Massey, all from Indiana; and Lerner, Congressman Yates, Will, and I from the Draft Committee.[1]

I opened the meeting by describing what we had accomplished up to that point. I then stressed that the reason we had called this meeting was to select a floor leader and someone to place Stevenson's name in nomination.

By this hour Stevenson's speech of welcome to the delegates, to be delivered on the following day, had been released to the pressroom, where we had secured a copy. Myers read it aloud to the group. There were nods of approval as it was being read and general agreement that this would stir the Convention.

"I'm satisfied," said Hoosier Governor Schricker.

Hubert Will then said that our delegate figures revealed a total of 178½ votes on the first ballot for Stevenson, a considerable jump over our calculations of the day before.

One of the Pennsylvania leaders asked how many votes we were counting on from Pennsylvania.

Will replied: "Thirty-five and a half."

The Pennsylvania leader remarked: "That's certainly accurate, because that's what the caucus just voted."

Will then explained that one of our volunteers had

[1] Archibald Alexander was not present as a result of a slip-up on the part of the individual assigned to notify him. Kenneth Anderson had a representative present. Both were immediately informed about the decisions made. Schricker had arrived in Chicago that day, and this was his first visit to our headquarters.

attended the caucus and phoned in the vote just as
Myers, Lawrence, and Finnegan arrived at our headquarters from their caucus.

In spite of the oppressive heat, the announcement
of the Pennsylvania vote—known only to Will and
the three Pennsylvania leaders—introduced a note of
strong optimism into the meeting. We all knew that
if Pennsylvania had failed to produce a sizable Stevenson vote, the draft efforts might die. Now we were
convinced that when the results of the vote of this
delegation from a leading industrial state were printed
in the newspapers the next day, the draft would gain
additional momentum. (A reporter for the *Baltimore
Sun* on the next day wrote: "Senator Estes Kefauver,
who must obtain large new blocs of delegates if his
candidacy is to advance, was searching for some way to
recover from the setback he received last night when a
poll of the 70 vote Pennsylvania delegation showed
32 delegates favoring Gov. Adlai Stevenson as com-
pared with 15½ votes for Kefauver." [2]

After the announcement of the Pennsylvania caucus vote, Schricker asked for our tabulation on Indiana.

Will said: "Twenty-five out of twenty-six because
one delegate is for Kefauver."

Schricker replied: "That's exactly right."

At this point in the meeting Finnegan suggested
that Mayor Lawrence might make the ideal floor
leader. Lawrence declined, however, saying: "You

[2] For some reason the newspapers reported only 32 Stevenson
votes at the Pennsylvania caucus. Our records and those of James A.
Finnegan reveal that the correct figure was 35½—just a majority.
Our figures also show only 14½ for Kefauver, in second position in
the caucus.

need a man with more vitamins than I've got to do the floor work." He recommended Myers. In view of former Senator Myers's record as majority whip in the Senate, and the fact that he knew and was respected by both Northern and Southern leaders of the party, all those present immediately supported Lawrence's suggestion.

With this solved, the group moved to the question of the man to place Stevenson's name in nomination. Lawrence looked at Schricker and said: "Governor, you should do it."

Since our Draft Committee had been urging Schricker to do this for days, we were most happy to have the pressure now come from Pennsylvania.

Schricker at first demurred. He said that we must know whether Stevenson would accept if the nomination was offered him. A number of those present objected and insisted that no one must ask the Governor if he could nominate him. Then Schricker said he wanted to talk it over with some members of his delegation in the morning and would let us know the next day.

We then adjourned with an agreement to meet at four p.m. the next day. And our committee was assigned the responsibility of inviting additional leaders to the Monday meeting.

Doris Fleeson caught the momentum that the draft movement had achieved by Sunday, the 20th, when she wrote in her column (*Washington Star*, July 21): "It now looks as though Gov. Adlai Stevenson will be dragged protesting to the presidential altar by the Democratic party. His shrieks are growing fainter. His suitor more importunate."

CHAPTER VIII

THE OPENING DAY OF THE
CONVENTION: MONDAY,
JULY 21

A few minutes after the Convention convened, the draft movement gained solid support from an unexpected source—Stevenson himself.

When he stepped up to the rostrum to welcome the Convention to Illinois, his appearance set off wild applause for about six minutes. Then, as Reston wrote in the *New York Times*, "The 'reluctant candidate,' who has been trying to talk himself out of the Democratic Presidential nomination for the last five months, talked himself right into the leading candidate's role this morning with a fifteen-minute address that impressed the convention from left to right. . . ."

This able speech contributed to the growing draft movement. Had he delivered a dull, pedantic talk, the reaction might have stalled the draft machinery. But the speech, sparkling with humor, with insight, with good frank common sense, and with catchy phrases, stirred the Convention. As it played an important role in the draft—though unexpected as far as Stevenson himself was concerned—the speech is reprinted here in full:

Mr. Chairman, Delegates and Guests of the convention: I thought I came here to greet you, not you to greet me. I am grateful for your courtesy, but I have an assignment here this morning as Governor of the host state to welcome the 1952 Democratic convention. And, in the name of 9,000,000 people of Illinois, I extend to you the heartiest of greetings.

Chicago and Illinois are proud that once again the party conventions by which we restate our principles and choose our candidates for the greatest temporal office on earth are held here at Chicago at the crossroads of the continent.

Here, my friends, on the prairies of Illinois and of the Middle West we can see a long way in all directions. We look to East, to West, to North and South. Our commerce, our ideas, come and go in all directions.

Here there are no barriers, no defenses, to ideas and to aspirations. We want none; we want no shackles on the mind or the spirit, no rigid patterns of thought, and no iron conformity. We want only the faith and the conviction that triumph in free and fair contest.

As a Democrat perhaps you will permit me to remind you that until four years ago the people of Illinois had chosen but three Democratic Governors in a hundred years. One was John Peter Altgeld, whom the great Illinois poet, Vachel Lindsay called the Eagle Forgotten. He was an immigrant. One was Edward F. Dunne, whose parents came from the old sod of Ireland, and last was Henry Horner, but one generation removed from Germany. John Peter Altgeld, my friends, was a Protestant, Governor Dunne was a Catholic, Henry Horner was a Jew.

And that, my friends, is the American story, written by the Democratic party here on the prairies of Illinois.

You are very welcome here in the heartland of the nation. Indeed, we think that you were wise to come here for your deliberations in this fateful year of grace. For it was in Chicago that the modern Democratic story began. It was here just twenty years ago this month in the depths of shattering national misery at the end of a dizzy decade of Republican rule that you commenced the greatest era of economic and social progress in our history.

It was here, my friends, in Chicago just twenty years ago this month that you nominated Franklin Roosevelt; twenty years during which we have fought total depression to victory and have never been more prosperous; twenty years during which we have fought total war to victory, both East and West, and have launched the United Nations—history's most ambitious experiment in international security; twenty years, my friends, that close now in the grim contest with the Communist conspiracy on every continent.

But our Republican friends have said that it was all a miserable failure. For almost a week pompous phrases marched over this landscape in search of an idea, and the only idea they found was that the two great decades of progress in peace, and of victory in war, and of bold leadership in this anxious hour, were the misbegotten spawn of bungling, of corruption, of socialism, of mismanagement, of waste and of worse. They captured, they tied and they dragged that ragged idea here into this hall and they furiously beat it to death for a solid week.

After listening to this everlasting procession of epithets about our misdeeds I was even surprised the next morning when the mail was delivered on time. I guess our Republican friends were out of patience, out of sorts, and need I add, out of office.

But we Democrats were by no means the only victims here. First, they slaughtered each other and then they went after us. And the same vocabulary was good for both exercises, which was a great convenience. Perhaps the proximity of the stockyards accounts for the carnage.

My friends, the constructive spirit of the two great Democratic decades must not die here on its twentieth anniversary; they must not die here in destructive indignity and disorder. And I hope and pray, as you all do, that we can conduct our deliberations with a businesslike precision and a dignity befitting our responsibility and the solemnity of the hour in history in which we meet.

For it is a very solemn hour indeed, freighted with the hopes and the fears of millions of mankind who seek in us, the Democratic party, sober understanding of the breadth and depth of the revolutionary currents in the world. Here and abroad they see in us awareness that there is no turning back, and that, as Justice Holmes said, "We must sail sometimes with the wind, sometimes against it; but we must sail and not drift or lie at anchor." They see in us, the Democratic party that has steered this country through a storm of spears for twenty years, an understanding of a world in the torment of transition from an age that has died to an age struggling to be born. They see in us relentless determination to stand fast against the barbarian at the gate, to cultivate allies with a decent respect for the opinion of others, to patiently explore every misty path to peace and security which is the only certainty of lower taxes and a better life.

This is not the time for superficial solutions and for endless elocution, this is not the time for frantic boasts and foolish words. For words are not deeds and there are no cheap and painless solutions to war, to hunger, to ignorance, to fear and to the new imperialism of the Soviet Union. My friends, you know full well that intemperate criticism is not a policy for the nation; and denunciation is not a program for our salvation. Words that are calculated to catch everyone may catch no one. And I hope that we can profit from their mistakes not just for our partisan benefit but for the benefit of all of us, Republicans and Democrats alike.

Where we have erred, let there be no denial; and where we have wronged the public trust, let there be no excuses. Self-criticism is the secret weapon of democracy, and candor and confession are good for the political soul. But we will never appease, we will never apologize for our leadership of the great events of this critical century all the way from Woodrow Wilson to Harry Truman.

We glory rather in these imperishable pages of our country's chronicle. But a great record of past achievement is not good enough. There can be no complacency perhaps for years to come. We dare not just look back to great yesterdays. We must look forward to great tomorrows.

What counts now is not just what we are against, but what we are for. And who leads us is less important than what leads us—what convictions, what courage, what faith —win or lose. A man does not save a century or a civilization, but a militant party wedded to a principle can.

So I hope that our preoccupation here is not just with personalities but with objectives. And I hope that the spirit of this convention is a confident reaffirmation that the United States is strong, resolved, resourceful and rich; that we know our duty and the destiny of this Heaven-rescued land; that we can and we will pursue a strong, consistent, honorable policy abroad, and meanwhile preserve the free institutions of life and of commerce at home.

What America needs and what the world wants is not bombast, abuse and double talk, but a sober message of firm faith and of confidence. St. Francis said: "Where there is patience and humility there is neither anger nor worry." And that might well be our text.

And let us remember that we are not meeting here alone. All the world is watching and listening to what we say, what we do and how we behave. So let us give them a demonstration of democracy in action at its best—our manners good, our proceedings orderly and dignified— and, above all, let us make our decisions openly, fairly, not by the processes of synthetic excitement or mass hysteria. Let us make them as these solemn times demand, by earnest thought and by prayerful deliberation.

And thus can the people's party reassure the people and vindicate and strengthen the forces of democracy throughout the world. Thank you.

The speech itself demonstrated Stevenson's pre-eminence as a public figure. It had the same notable quality that was to characterize his campaign speeches. When he finished, the Convention again burst into vigorous and sustained applause until Stevenson brought it to a close by leaving the rostrum.

There was no organ music and no marching up and down the aisles, thus attesting to the spontaneous nature of the demonstration.

As the Alsops wrote in their column:

. . . The force of the grass roots sentiment among the delegates was plainly evident in the reception accorded to Stevenson when he made his speech of welcome. "Spontaneous demonstrations," with cheer leaders, organizers and demonstrators paid $5 an hour, have become a tiresome joke at our quadrennial political rallies. This demonstration for Stevenson was wholly unorganized. It made less noise than the planned and paid-for type. But it expressed real feeling. . . .

Shortly after the speech, we were besieged by many delegates who had not visited our headquarters before. One California delegate arrived half an hour after Stevenson had finished and said: "That settles it. Stevenson is the only man I can support. You know I had never seen him before and I didn't realize how wonderful he is." In spite of this outburst of enthusiasm, California remained committed to Kefauver. Growing Stevenson sentiment in the delegation, however, made it increasingly restless.

The Convention response to Stevenson's performance created an atmosphere of exhilaration when our draft meeting took place at four p.m. Now many uncommitted delegates, and the TV and radio audience, knew why we were so adamant in proceeding with the draft of a man who was not a candidate.

Since our headquarters was swarming with reporters, we held this Monday meeting a few blocks away from the hotel in the Chicago Loop law office of Congressman Yates. Present at the meeting were Myers and Finnegan of Pennsylvania, Schricker and Butler of Indiana, Anderson and John Young of Kansas, Jonathan Daniels of North Carolina, Alexander of New Jersey, Joe Gluck, National Committeeman from the state of Washington, and Lerner, Yates, and I.[1]

[1] In addition to those mentioned in the text of this book the following delegates or influential people were most helpful in the draft: Barney L. Whatley of Colorado; La Fayette Patterson of Alabama; John Lane and John M. Bailey of Connecticut; Gilbert Larsen of Idaho; R. W. Baxter, M. P. Hogan, and Lex Hawkins of Iowa; F. Davis Clark and E. S. Muskie of Maine; John Nangle and Willa Mae Roberts of Missouri; Dwight Palmer, Mr. and Mrs. Thorn Lord, and Mayor George Brunner of New Jersey; William D. Carlebach, Otis G. Pike, and Jesse R. Sharlette of New York; Frank R. Hutton of North Carolina; Robert J. Bulkley, James Shocknessy, and Howard M. Metzenbaum of Ohio; Monroe Sweetland and Dave Epps of Oregon; Senator John O. Pastore of Rhode Island; Sanford

I chairmaned the meeting and summarized the discussion of the night before. I mentioned that our delegate count on the first ballot remained the same as it had been yesterday—178½ votes.

Daniels interjected that he was convinced Stevenson would accept a draft.

I then turned to Schricker and said: "Governor, will you nominate Stevenson?"

With no hesitation Schricker replied: "Yes, I will."

Alexander, who was sitting next to him, took hold of Schricker's shoulder and said: "Governor, you are doing a wonderful thing!" Myers and the others present immediately echoed Alexander's statement.

Schricker then went on to say that at a breakfast for the Democratic governors that morning, he had talked a bit with Stevenson. Although the Illinois Governor had reiterated that he was a candidate only for governor, Schricker told us: "I am now convinced that Stevenson would not refuse a draft." [2]

We then agreed to release to the press that evening the announcement of Myers as floor leader. The following day, to give additional impetus to a bandwagon psychology, we would announce Schricker as the man who was to place Stevenson's name in nomination.

Petersky, Jim Wilson, and John Goldmark of Washington; and Okey L. Patterson and William G. Changes, Jr., of West Virginia.

[2] Later that day when queried by the press, Schricker said: "My feeling is that he will accept a draft." On July 22 the newspapers carried the following statement from Stevenson: "I have not seen nor talked with Gov. Schricker since breakfast time yesterday. I have no comment on his reported statement except to say I told him I wanted to run again for governor of Illinois and I hoped he would help me to do so."

At this point Myers stated that if Stevenson phoned him to try to persuade him to cease his efforts as floor leader, he would refuse to do so.[3]

The group agreed that nothing should come from anyone in the draft movement on the question of the vice-presidential nominee. In the first place, this would be Stevenson's decision. Moreover, it had been our strategy to ignore publicly any discussion of the rivals for the nomination. We certainly did not want to appear to be putting any evaluation on any candidates, one as against another.

Then Myers and Finnegan insisted that it was best for all groups represented at the meeting to work from the Draft Stevenson Committee headquarters at the Hilton Hotel. The Draft Committee should continue to interview delegates and project the votes ballot by ballot. Myers, as floor leader, would confine his efforts to key people in each delegation. As floor leader, he would also be the contact man with party leaders like Arvey.

It was also agreed that the Draft Committee would place an order immediately for fifteen hundred placards with sticks attached, with the slogan "America Needs Stevenson." At this point the group expressed its agreement with the policy already adopted by our committee of not sponsoring any noisy parades and

[3] The New York Post, July 22, said that Stevenson, on hearing that Myers had become floor leader, said: "I have sent word to Myers that I hope he will discontinue his activity." Arvey urged Myers to cease his activities as floor leader, but Myers did not know whether Arvey was speaking for Stevenson or not. Myers had never met Stevenson and did not meet him until after Stevenson's acceptance speech. Myers knew all the other contenders quite well, which placed him in a somewhat embarrassing personal situation.

demonstrations through the corridors of the Hilton Hotel.

Myers remarked that Senator J. W. Fulbright of Arkansas had told him he liked the fact that the whole Draft Stevenson movement had been characterized by dignity.

Just before the meeting adjourned, we of the Draft Committee suggested that since Myers had become the floor leader he should be chairman of future meetings of the group.

Myers replied: "Nothing doing. You have done an excellent job. Your committee has done an amazing piece of work with the press and the delegates. It must be an important part of the continuing picture. None of us who are delegates want the Citizen's Committee out of the picture." [4]

"I endorse those sentiments entirely," Alexander commented.

News of our meeting quickly leaked to the press. In fact, by the time we returned to the Hilton, reporters were clamoring for a statement.[5] We fended them off

[4] *Newsweek*, August 4, 1952, stressed how Lawrence, Myers, and Schricker "agreed to work with the Committee, instead of taking command of the Stevenson movement themselves." In a conversation with me in 1954, Myers and Finnegan explained their decision to work with the Draft Stevenson Committee in this way. They liked what the committee had already accomplished. In view of the Governor's adamant stand, they felt they could not alone launch a draft. The Draft Stevenson Committee, therefore, was a functioning vehicle through which they could work.

[5] Howard Norton, for instance, said in the *Baltimore Sun*: ". . . While the corridors hummed with talk of the demonstration accorded Stevenson when he rose to make his welcoming speech to the convention this afternoon, things of a more practical nature were going on behind closed doors.

"Leaders of the draft-Stevenson movement accelerated their

until Myers issued the following statement through our press office:

Last night at the Pennsylvania delegation meeting, it was conclusively decided that Governor Stevenson is the choice of the convention. In our opinion, this is a true reflection of the sentiments of the country at large.

Following that decision, a group of delegates representing 25 states asked us to assist in the Draft Stevenson movement. This magnificent coordination is the result of the tireless and at one time lonesome persistence of the National Committee, Stevenson for President. They had a firm belief, and will soon see theirs, mine and the country's desire fully realized.

The request that has been made of me is to become floor leader in the Draft Stevenson movement. I am not only pleased, as would be the case in any normal convention of this great party. But this is not normal. It is therefore not only a pleasure, but truly an honor for me.

---

planning of the moves needed to put the Governor's name in nomination. . . ."

CHAPTER IX

THE STEVENSON BANDWAGON ROLLS: TUESDAY, JULY 22

By THE second day of the Convention all the efforts of the past week reached a focus in a fast-moving Stevenson bandwagon. The *Chicago Sun-Times* featured:

STEVENSON HEADLINES ACROSS NATION
From coast to coast newspapers seem agreed on the Gov. Stevenson story as is apparent from the headlines reprinted here:

ILLINOIS WILL IGNORE STEVENSON'S "NO"—N.Y. *Times*
NEW STEVENSON "NO," BUT THE BOOM GOES ON—N.Y. *Herald Tribune*
GOV. STEVENSON BOOM ZOOMS—N.Y. *Daily News*
STEVENSON BOOM IN FULL SWING—N.Y. *Journal American*
STEVENSON BOOM STILL ON—N.Y. *Post*
STEVENSON DRAFT PICKS UP STEAM—Washington *Post*
PRESSURE MOUNTS TO DRAFT STEVENSON—Washington *Star*
DRAFT STEVENSON MOVE IS PLANNED—San Francisco *Chronicle*
"DRAFT" OF STEVENSON ON—San Francisco *Examiner*
STEVENSON GETS 32 PA. VOTES—Nashville *Tennessean*
STEVENSON BOOM STILL ON—Boston *Globe*
STEVENSON GAINING AS BARKLEY SLIPS—Baltimore *News-Post*
STEVENSON BEGS OFF, BUT BACKERS TALK DRAFT—Cleveland *Plain Dealer*

Leading reporters emphasized how Stevenson's speech of welcome had stirred the Convention. And the news stories described the selection of Myers as the floor leader of the draft.

Roscoe Drummond said in the *Christian Science Monitor:*

. . . There is ascending, almost crescendo determination to nominate the reluctant candidate. Unless Gov. Adlai E. Stevenson hires a B-36 and sky writes a signed affidavit saying more than General Sherman—that he will not accept even if unanimously nominated and will not serve even if unanimously elected, positively—few observers give this convention more than two or three ballots to reach its decision. . . .

The *Boston Globe* said in an editorial:

Adlai Stevenson's reluctance to be drafted for the Democratic presidential nomination seems to make him only the more attractive. Certainly the emergence of the Illinois Governor as the hope of a party beset with too many candidates is the most significant fact of the Democratic convention so far. . . .

And Raymond P. Brandt said in the *St. Louis Post-Dispatch:*

. . . By a miracle greater than that which enabled Wendell Willkie to snatch the 1940 Republican standard from Gov. Thomas E. Dewey and Senator Robert A. Taft, the 52-year-old Governor has been the beneficiary of a situation in which the draft notice is catching up with him while he is running away from it. . . . Unsolicited, the nomination appears to be his for the taking. It will be another miracle if it is not formally presented to him by the convention.

These favorable news stories, and others, were quickly reproduced by us and distributed to the delegates on Tuesday.

By midmorning the fifteenth floor of the Hilton Hotel was swarming with activity. As one reporter said, our headquarters "was full of bounce today. Volunteers were crawling over each other to help spread the Stevenson gospel." And Seymour Freidin said in the *New York Post* (July 25):

Delegates, hat in hand, are coming to them in droves and par-boiled old politicians are beating on the doors of their headquarters to ask if they can get in on the act.

Only a few weeks ago, Stevenson workers were scoffed at as starry-eyed do-gooders chasing a rainbow. They wanted to nominate and elect a man for President who wouldn't even acknowledge them.

Now they are regarded as clever makers of a modern miracle, their work is envied by the opposition as the most daring play attempted in recent national politics if it works.

"Gotta hand it to them," one politician remarked, "they're parlaying a name into the Presidency. Very smart."

Early on the 22nd we expanded to fourteen rooms, ordered many phones installed, and tightened up on the orderliness of the headquarters. With the assistance of R. Sargent Shriver, Jr., close friend of Congressman John Kennedy of Massachusetts, a number of Andy Frain's uniformed ushers were hired and an around-the-clock squad of city detectives were assigned to assist in maintaining order among the crowds circulating in the foyer by the elevators.

By Tuesday the draft was moving so well that we no longer had difficulty in securing contributions.

Before this happy situation occurred, an occasional friend by writing us a check made a real contribution to our activities. One day a personal friend of mine, John L. Leban of New York City, visiting Chicago on business, read of my activities in the papers. He and his son, Howard, came to visit our headquarters. He is a very successful business executive; his son was then a college student. After looking our headquarters over and asking us how much money we had to spend or had spent, Leban remarked: "I don't see how you do it—an operation like this takes thousands of dollars!" His son casually replied: "Dad, it's simple, they do it with mirrors!" With that, his father wrote a generous check, saying, as he handed it to me: "This is to help keep the mirrors polished."

These expressions from time to time became lost in the context of the tenseness and confusion of the operation as a whole. But they certainly were great morale-builders, and compensated for the heartaches that lack of money caused.

We deposited in the bank from February through the end of the Convention a total of $20,300.91. We ended with a favorable balance of $507.13, which was contributed to the Stevenson Presidential campaign.[1]

In the course of all this hectic activity, we were experiencing something entirely new to some of us: the mechanics and hocus-pocus of a convention headquarters. There were ardent advocates of more

[1] Letter from George Overton to U.S. Senate Subcommittee on Privileges and Elections, January 9, 1953.

"causes" and "interests" than any of us had ever heard of. There were personalities and characters who seemed to step right out of fiction. There were "tipsters," "dopesters," and "experts." There were big shots and little shots from back home.

Then there was the chairman of a state delegation who promised to deliver his whole state's vote on the second ballot. A heartening promise, assuredly. But the primary laws of his state governed otherwise.

There were "observers." We had much fun with this category. These were the folks who came around in the "interest" of other candidates, and who "reported back" all they could learn about our activities. This is the "traditional spy system" of political conventions, the "cops and robbers" game of learning the other fellow's strategy. To say the least, they were interesting people.

We, too, had means of learning what was going on in other camps. You don't always have to plan for it; it is many times volunteered. Not that any of the information or "strategy" being worked out elsewhere could seriously affect what we were doing; nevertheless, we were kept informed whether we wanted to be or not.

Never a dull moment—for there is no one more talkative than a zealous political volunteer, and we had them on all sides.

Perhaps a little anecdote will illustrate how casually we took this business of "observers."

After the traffic became heavy on our fifteenth floor we established stations at various places in the foyer and corridors which were to stop unidentifiable people from passing. It served also to expedite visitors to the person whom they had come to see. We were not playing "hard to see"; we were just trying to keep a little order amid mobs of people. This had its drawbacks too. As with any such group staffed with volunteers, some people were turned away who should not have been. The experienced and hardy, however, tried again until they succeeded.

One day a personable young man came to our outer office and presented himself as a volunteer who wished to do whatever was assigned to him. He was given one of the screening posts—one quite close to the suite in which I was working. He was brought in and introduced to me. I welcomed him and went about doing what his visit had interrupted. He performed his duties well. The detective sergeant in charge of the police squad said that, if nothing else, the young man was always at his post.

The reason? When he got off the elevator, he was immediately identified as a worker in one of the other headquarters. The staff member who assigned him to his post with us phoned to me that this was so, but that I should not indicate we knew who he was when he was introduced.

This certainly was one way to let our opposition know what was going on in our headquarters. We had no secrets. Our entire effort was to let everybody possible know what we were doing; that what we said about the Stevenson draft was backed up with delegate votes.

On midmorning of the 22nd the Stevenson leaders in the Pennsylvania delegation moved in with us to work from our headquarters whenever they were not on the Convention floor. Myers, Finnegan, Teefy, John A. Hayes, William Foster, former assistant to Myers in the Senate, Joseph McLaughlin, public-relations man, and Helen Lukiewski were among those working from the Hilton headquarters.

Immediately, over the signature of Myers as floor leader, we sent telegrams to every National Committeeman and state chairman asking for their support of the Stevenson draft.

Congressman John Kennedy, too, joined us and worked to organize for the draft candidates campaigning for the Senate and the House of Representatives. Michael DiSalle, campaigning against Senator Bricker in Ohio, joined forces with Kennedy on these plans. They felt that a little prod from candidates might help convince Stevenson of the party's need for him. They themselves were facing extremely difficult contests and figured that Stevenson was the only Democratic contender whose name at the top of the ticket would help carry them to victory.

That evening—through our committee—Kennedy, DiSalle, Congressman Walter Granger of Utah, and Alexander of New Jersey called upon other Democratic leaders to sign the following statement:

The great popular movement to Draft Governor Adlai E. Stevenson which started in Illinois is now spreading to the entire nation. As Democrats from widely different sections of the country, we endorse this inspiring demonstration of grass roots democracy at its best. We call upon our fellow Democrats to select this great governor as our nominee for the presidency.

We arranged that Will, Holleb, and Ming, in charge of our records on delegates, would prepare at regular intervals the latest tally on delegate votes. We, also took steps to ensure that this tally, state by state, could be sent to Myers on the floor of the Convention. It was agreed that Myers, Finnegan, Alexander, and Anderson of Kansas would work principally from the floor of the Convention, rounding up delegate votes.

Before the Convention opened, as I have written, we had rented a room in the Stock Yards Inn and had installed a direct wire for such an eventuality. Volunteers were stationed in this room whenever the Convention was in session to relay messages between the Hilton and the Convention floor. This phone became so burdened, however, that we secured the co-operation of Andy Frain and the Bell Telephone Company. They allowed us to phone messages to their respective offices just off the Convention floor, where our volunteers were waiting to take them to Lou Alexander, one of our key volunteers, who then carried them into the Convention.

We had some difficulty at first in getting our people on the floor of the Convention. Since we were not recognized by the Democratic National Committee, they allocated no badges or passes to us. Yates had his Congressman's badge and this allowed him to circulate freely. And the Pennsylvania delegation loaned us the badges of a sergeant at arms and an alternate, and the liaison between the floor and the hotel became effective.

Many of these messages conveyed information

about changes in various delegations as a result of caucuses, which were being held with great frequency. Days before the Convention opened, we had assigned a volunteer—usually a lawyer or a war veteran—to each state and territorial delegation.[2]

In a number of cases, the delegations were quite willing to have our volunteer associate with them. A schoolteacher, Anna G. Pickens, assigned to Mississippi, though she got nowhere votewise, later informed us that she had been taken to dinner, allowed to sit in on caucuses, and made an "honorary" member of the delegation.

After we had formed our coalition with Pennsylvania, Indiana, New Jersey, and Kansas, one reporter stated that the Draft Stevenson Committee had now "bowed out" of the draft movement. Others described how "professionals" had now "moved in" on the draft. When we had opened our headquarters some writers seemed to be critical of the "amateurishness" of the operation. But now, when we had joined with delegates who had votes, we were under attack for becoming "professional"!

By Tuesday a number of leaders not active the previous week in the draft movement had begun jumping on the bandwagon.

The night before, Vice-President Barkley issued a statement dramatically withdrawing his candidacy. He said caustically:

[2] Included in this group were Lou Alexander, Joseph Minsky, Milton Mallin, Herbert Grossberg, Homer Johanson, George Watson, John Clay, Victor Stone, Milton Cohen, Fred Vosse, Joe Brunswick, Dorothy Roberts, Calvin Hoyt, Donald Yellon, Robert Hunt, and Morris H. Hirsh.

I would be derelict in my responsibility to the American people and to myself if I failed to state the reasons which caused me to withdraw my name from the consideration of the convention.

I shall state them now. It has always been my belief, and my record supports this, that the Democratic party should serve without favor the best interests of all segments of our life, the rich, the poor, the Negro, the Jew, the Catholic, the Protestant, the laborer in the field, the laborer in the factory, the business man, the farmer, and the oppressed, wherever they may be.

I have never believed, and do not now believe, that any one of these groups should be permitted to dominate or control either of the great political parties of our nation.

However, since arriving in Chicago, I have learned that certain self-anointed political labor leaders have taken it upon themselves to announce their opposition to me as the Democratic nominee for President. They have admitted to me that weeks ago they committed themselves to a program and to candidates other than myself, which would give them greater control of the machinery and policies of the Democratic party.

At the same time, the leaders of certain large delegations, who have been encouraging my candidacy, now find it expedient to withdraw their proffered support of me. . . .

Ten C.I.O. and A.F.L. leaders, including Jack Kroll, Walter Reuther, and Joseph Keenan, had told the Vice-President on Monday morning the 21st that they could not support him.[3] Later that day these leaders made the announcement public. They also announced

[3] See Alben Barkley's autobiography, *That Reminds Me* (New York: Doubleday & Co.; 1954), for a detailed description of this incident.

that they were supporting Averell Harriman or Senator Kefauver, though they admitted there was a "good deal of Stevenson sentiment" among the two hundred Convention delegates who were members of these organizations.

One hour after Mr. Barkley's withdrawal, the Associated Press called to ask if we had a statement to issue. We said: "No. We are sorry to see that he had to withdraw under such circumstances." "Aren't you jubilant?" the AP man asked? "No, not in the least," we replied.

Following the Barkley announcement we were faced with a need for analyzing its causes and effects. Frankly, we had not anticipated this. We had anticipated such statements from two of the other candidates, but not from Barkley. The withdrawal was certainly a factor that had great significance. It seemed to us that these labor leaders had opposed the Vice-President because of a struggle for power within the party. Approaching it from this conclusion, we reviewed some of the critical cracks in the party's internal structure.

It was generally known that since the Convention in 1948, the issue of North-South feelings on FEPC had become one important factor in the alignment of some of the delegates behind Russell, Kefauver, and Harriman for the '52 Convention. And it was without question the one issue that could create a deadlock in the Convention.

Several days before Barkley's withdrawal, our monitoring service had fully reported a broadcast by Eric Sevareid of CBS. He had pointed out that the "arithmetic" of this Convention could not add up to a majority for any of the candidates. He reasoned that because of the issues that had to be compromised, no candidate could compromise far enough from stated policy to satisfy both his own following and a compromise following sufficient to poll a majority. He reasoned that when the time for nominations and balloting arrived, the delegates would come to the conclusion that Stevenson was the only person who could secure the votes from the compromise states.

His logic was calculating, clear, convincing, and conclusive. So much so that his phrase "the arithmetic of the convention" had been adopted into the language we were using in our explanations.

Now, the Barkley withdrawal brought Sevareid's arithmetic into the forefront of our thinking.

The "Labor Breakfast" that brought about Barkley's withdrawal was reported to us with as many variations as there were people present. The significant factor, however, was that it had caused the withdrawal. We had nothing but meager reports, none of which could be substantially verified; so we projected logic. The fact that the breakfast attendance was not a complete representation of labor indicated that the breakfast really did not represent labor delegates as a whole —and that no one could speak for labor as a whole.

All of this narrowed down to the fact that the spark causing the fire must have been set off by a faction that wanted to eliminate him—perhaps because of his age, but also perhaps as an issue or a symbol. For it was quite likely that Barkley could have been the candidate around whom the pending issue of the North-

South split could be rallied. But this could be accomplished only by a capitulation of the extreme Northern liberals. And they would have no part of that, we reasoned, as it would have threatened their having real power in the Convention.

This thought was strengthened in our minds by this sentence in the Vice-President's statement of withdrawal:

They have admitted to me that weeks ago they committed themselves to a program and to candidates other than myself, which would give them greater control of the machinery and policies of the Democratic party.

With this as our reasoning, our basic strategy was simple. We carried on with our original intention of giving the delegates the facts of an uncontrolled Convention. We had kept silent on the struggles for power within the party factions. Our only reference to them was an occasional observation that the Convention had a responsibility to prevent capture of the party machinery by a faction that intended to convert it to its own design regardless of party and the national interest. But beginning Tuesday, we stressed this idea more frequently.

There naturally was much speculation in the press about the Barkley withdrawal. The Alsops, in their July 23 column, observed that when Stevenson refused to be a candidate Senate Secretary Leslie Biffle and other leaders had gone all out for the Vice-President. The White House also encouraged Barkley to become an active candidate, as did Arvey.

The Alsops flatly stated that Arvey, Mayor Lawrence, and Governor Schricker were willing to give initial support to the Vice-President. If he failed to be nominated and a deadlock occurred, then they meant to draft Stevenson. This report left us bewildered by the inclusion of Lawrence and Schricker. They were active in the Stevenson draft before Barkley's withdrawal, as their participation in the July 20 meeting we had called demonstrated. At this meeting, too, they had committed themselves to drafting Stevenson before a deadlock could occur.[4]

We knew that on Sunday, the 20th, Frank McKinney, Chairman of the National Committee, had told several delegations that President Truman hoped and desired that the Vice-President would be nominated. The Barkley strategists themselves that night announced publicly that the President was for Barkley. The Alsops wrote that this statement stimulated "a violent countersurge among the delegates. The delegates wished to win, thought the Democratic party could win but did not believe the party could win with a seventy-four-year-old standard bearer."

This surge among the delegates was encouraged by the determination of younger candidates for office such as Alexander and younger party leaders like Finnegan and Myers, who favored the more youthful Stevenson. Their lack of interest in the Barkley

[4] As further information on this point, Schricker wrote to me on April 10, 1954: ". . . I was never committed or even solicited to support Mr. Barkley . . . I declared myself for Stevenson early in 1952, and so informed at least three other candidates during their pre-convention visits to our State. Kerr, Kefauver and Harriman can confirm this statement. If Governor Stevenson had declined the nomination then most of Indiana's delegates, including myself, would have supported Barkley, had he remained in the race."

candidacy was quite different from that of the ten labor leaders representing a faction. Stevenson, like the Vice-President, was the leader of a broad coalition, not the spokesman of a faction. Those involved in the Stevenson draft wanted a man whose interests reflected a broad view of the nation as a whole, who had an appeal beyond parochial factionalism, and who was also a youthful, vigorous, proved vote-getter.[5]

There is no doubt that the Barkley withdrawal hastened the bandwagon move to Stevenson. As Paul R. Leach said in the *Chicago Daily News* on Tuesday: "Stevenson had been a strong probability from the beginning of the convention. The draft movement was sent soaring shortly after midnight when Vice-President Barkley announced his withdrawal."

Governor Elbert N. Carvel of Delaware, after the Barkley announcement, said that he and most of his delegation had switched to Stevenson. Carvel added that he would like to make a seconding speech after Stevenson's name had been placed in nomination.

A few hours before the Vice-President's announcement, James A. Farley, a Barkley supporter, had told

[5] Lawrence wrote to me on April 15, 1954: ". . . I was working in close association with Mr. McKinney and received word, the Sunday week before the Convention that Washington was looking favorably upon Vice President Barkley. Senator Myers and I discussed the matter with a number of our leaders in the State, with the unanimous result that, to wit: 'we love Barkley and would like to see him President, but we are fearful that his age is against him, and that people will think if we nominate him that we are just making a nice gesture toward a Democratic "war horse."' That is possibly how the impression got abroad that we were carrying the torch for Barkley. I reported to McKinney that we could not get any real response from our delegates for the 'Veep.'"

reporters that he expected Stevenson to be nominated on an early ballot.[6] The next day Farley hustled aboard the Stevenson bandwagon, saying: "The people of this country—judging by the delegates here—want him. They feel that in this particular picture he fits in." [7]

An excellent example of the draft psychology at work occurred when a California delegate—a mayor of a city—came to our headquarters and said: "You've got a bandwagon here and I want to get on it."

We replied: "Fine but what about the California delegation?"

He said: "Well, we are bound by the unit rule to vote for Kefauver. But, if we can only end that, we want to get on your bandwagon."

Doris Fleeson reflected the draft psychology starting to sweep the Convention when she wrote in her syndicated column on the 22nd:

. . . Stevenson seems destined to make political history by achieving a presidential nomination strictly on his own terms.

It appears that he will be the object of a genuine draft on a very early ballot. He has made no commitments to any person, state or voting bloc. . . . He is under no obligation to the incumbent President of his own party.

Even his floor leader [Myers] is being forced to volun-

[6] This statement by Farley was immediately put on radio and TV. Our monitoring service phoned it in to our headquarters. At this point Leo Lerner was talking to an uncommitted delegate who made it clear he would not be for Stevenson unless he was sure Stevenson would accept the nomination. Lerner took the note that had just been handed him and gave it to the delegate. "O.K.," said the delegate, "if Farley thinks he will be nominated, I guess I will stop worrying about whether he will accept."

[7] *New York Post*, July 23.

teer his services. The politicos are plaintive and bewildered by turns. They are still confident he can catch General Eisenhower in his mousetrap which is consolation enough.

The Governor has accomplished this without loss of dignity and even an occasional joke at his own expense. . . .

By Tuesday the Stevenson draft had gained such momentum that the Illinois delegation became restive. Arvey and the rest of the Illinois delegation by default —or, more precisely, as a result of the personal plea of Stevenson to do nothing to promote his name—found themselves in the position that others had organized the Stevenson draft. Arvey kept his promise to Stevenson, but it was difficult in view of the pressures on him. Arvey, when informed of the July 21 meeting called by us at which Schricker had agreed to place Stevenson in nomination, told reporters: "In line with my personal promise to Governor Stevenson to do not one thing to advance a campaign for him, I would have nothing to do with such drives."

But, said John Madigan in the *Chicago Herald-American* (July 22), "Illinois' powerful delegation . . . was shaken up today with demands that it not be left at the post when the Gov. Stevenson presidential race gets off to a flying start. . . ."

And Charles B. Cleveland reported in the *Chicago Daily News* (July 24):

. . . troubles are brewing in Arvey's own delegation. . . . Joseph L. Gill, delegation Chairman, has indicated that he is not altogether happy with the way the draft movement unfolded. Arvey had counseled that Illinois withhold its Stevenson vote until the second ballot to knock out talk that the draft was prearranged. But Gill hinted that he would plunk the Illinois votes right off the bat.

By July 22, the draft pioneered by a group of Chicago citizens—who frequently in local politics had opposed the Chicago organization—in collaboration with the Pennsylvania, Indiana, New Jersey, and Kansas delegations, had reached such a point that Illinois delegates quite naturally felt that they would look silly not to be supporting their own Governor. On the other hand, Arvey was bound by his promise to Stevenson not to participate in such activities. He relates in his *Reporter* article that on the 22nd of July "leaders in our delegation began warning me that we would 'look silly' not to vote for our Governor on the first ballot." He adds that he phoned Stevenson the next day and told him he would be nominated because no candidate could rally sufficient delegate strength. When he asked him if he would accept if nominated, Stevenson refused to answer and repeated that he was a candidate for re-election as Governor and nothing else.

Our headquarters gave additional momentum to the Stevenson bandwagon on Tuesday afternoon the 22nd. Schricker, after discussing a draft of his nominating speech with two of the committee's volunteers who were assisting him—Maurice Rosenfield and Professor Harry Kalven, Jr., of the University of Chicago Law School—held a crowded press conference on the fifteenth floor of the Hilton to announce that he would place Stevenson's name in nomination.

Following the press conference, Reston said in the *New York Times:*

. . . The Illinois Governor, meanwhile, was just a leaf on the rising stream. . . . Throughout the day, delegates from more than thirty States checked in with former Senator Francis Myers of Pennsylvania, the draft-Stevenson floor manager. In almost every case they reported their delegations were breaking toward Mr. Stevenson.

. . . In these last forty-eight hours, Mr. Stevenson has evidently amended his own definition of an honest draft. Originally he thought an honest draft could come only after a deadlock in the convention, but since the movement in his name has kept rolling despite his repeated protests, he now has indicated to friends that the "circumstances have got beyond me, and I am not to blame for them."

Mr. Stevenson himself indicated both the nature of his own personal struggle over the question today and his conclusion when he referred reporters to Matthew xxvi, 39, for his answer to the draft movement. The Bible verse follows:

"O my Father, if it be possible, let this cup pass from me: nevertheless, not as I will, but as Thou Wilt."

If Mr. Stevenson were able to see the headquarters that has been established here by his well-wishers, he would probably have little doubt about the authenticity of the present draft. . . .

It no more resembles a professional political headquarters than Mr. Stevenson resembles a typical professional courthouse politician.

. . . But amateur as it is, this headquarters helped keep Mr. Stevenson's name before the convention in the days before the bandwagon started to roll.

CHAPTER X

PLACING STEVENSON'S NAME
IN NOMINATION:
WEDNESDAY, THURSDAY,
JULY 23-4

"IF GOV. STEVENSON wins the nomination, which now
seems likely and, indeed, inevitable, he will have won
it on his own," said Louis Bromfield in the Hearst
press on the third day of the convention.

By Wednesday morning, July 23rd, it was known
to the delegates that Indiana had just pledged 25 of
its 26 votes to Stevenson; New Jersey had caucused
and pledged 28 of its 32 votes to the Governor; and
the Illinois caucus pledged 46 votes for Stevenson, 3
for Kefauver, and 11 not indicated but expected to be
for Stevenson. The chairman of the Illinois delegation,
Joseph Gill, said: "We are not going to nominate or
second anybody. We're respecting Gov. Stevenson's
wishes in that regard."

On the third day of the Convention the Missouri
delegation jumped on the Stevenson bandwagon.
Sitting in this delegation was President Truman's
alternate, whose instructions to cast his vote for the
Vice-President had now become obsolete.

The day before, in the *Christian Science Monitor*,
Roscoe Drummond had pointed out:

. . . This convention is jelling so speedily, the prospect is that President Truman will have no opportunity to determine the presidential nominee—even if he could. . . . They say that Mr. Truman, who can recognize a trend as well as the next politician, is ready to give his favor to Governor Stevenson. The view here is that if he does not do so shortly, he will be waving at a bandwagon which has passed by.

The newspapers reported on the 23rd that Connecticut was ready to swing to Stevenson on the second ballot. We had known for days of the Stevenson strength in this delegation. The delegation was committed on the first ballot, however, to nominate and vote for Senator Brien McMahon.

Some delegates from the Rocky Mountain states announced that they were ready to shift if indications pointed to an early nomination. And the Maryland delegation reserved seats on the bandwagon when one delegate said: "Maryland will move quickly when this Stevenson thing really starts." And the chairman of the delegation, Congressman L. G. Sasscer, expressed the feeling of the delegation when he said: "He's made a good Governor, and I believe he will make a good President. A lot of the delegates like him very much. No one dislikes him." [1]

We knew from our volunteers attached to each delegation that a number of states not mentioned by the press also were becoming restless. Stevenson support was growing in New York, for instance, and the leadership was having a difficult time holding the state for Harriman.

[1] *Baltimore Sun,* July 23.

As the Stevenson draft continued its momentum on Wednesday, James Roosevelt, of the Kefauver forces, charged that it was all a deep-laid plot backed by bosses of the big city political machines.

In a press conference immediately following Roosevelt's, we pointed out that the boom was "uncontrolled, unbossed and unstoppable." Then we explained how, after the delegates had come to us for information, we—not "city bosses"—had taken the lead in calling the two meetings that led to the organization of the draft machinery.

The Stevenson bandwagon was rolling so well on Wednesday night that at least one of the recent passengers decided to take over. This we learned from a series of events and circumstances which called into action our best efforts and reasoning.

During Wednesday evening, July 23, the crowds that had been around our headquarters—together with many of our committee—had gone down to the Convention hall. There the action of the draft movement centered on the floor leadership.

Those of us at the Hilton headquarters had an opportunity to relax, for the first evening since we had opened up. About eleven o'clock I was sitting with a few newspapermen and Joe McLaughlin from Philadelphia. We had been settling the problems of the world. I decided to go to bed.

Shortly after one o'clock Thursday morning, when the "watch" staff members on the fifteenth floor were Ann Ewing and Maureen Flanagan, Paul Butler, National Committeeman elect, of Indiana, stepped from the elevator into an almost darkened foyer. He asked for me and was told I had turned in. Actually, only one person knew what room I was in. And after Butler identified himself, I was awakened.

I met him in the front suite, which was the coolest of the quarters we were using. It was oppressively hot at best; there was no breeze even though we had four windows facing Lake Michigan. He immediately gave me a description of what had taken place at the Convention hall just an hour earlier. At this point Stuart Haydon returned from a walk and joined the conference. Butler gave us a detailed account of what had occurred.

About midnight, he said, on the floor of the Convention, Arvey had said to Schricker: "You're not going to nominate him are you? He doesn't want it." Schricker replied that he would make his own decision in the matter.

Arvey then said: "Didn't the Governor ask you not to do it?" Schricker replied: "No, he didn't. Adlai Stevenson said to me: 'I don't want you to do it but I can't stop you.'"

Then Butler reported that Arvey added: "Well, Stevenson asked Governor Carvel of Delaware not to nominate him. Will you please make it clear to Adlai that I had nothing to do with your decision to nominate him?"

Arvey then said: "Don't you know that Carvel is going to nominate him? Delaware comes ahead of Indiana on the roll-call. Anyway, if you nominate him, with Indiana being Illinois' neighbor, it will look like a put-up job."

Schricker replied: "My nominating him is not a

put-up job, and I am saying so in my speech."

They broke up, with Avery suggesting that they all meet at the Convention office a half hour before the next day's session to settle who would place Stevenson's name in nomination.

Immediately, Schricker tried to reach Carvel on the phone. That call and many others throughout the night went unanswered.

We decided we must prevent this apparent Arvey-Carvel arrangement from taking place. It was not that we had any personal objection to Carvel, but if he placed Stevenson's name in nomination, this would not represent the broad coalition of forces and individuals which had organized and developed the draft movement.

Our floor leader, Myers, was from an Eastern industrial state. The man to make the nomination speech, we felt, should come from a Midwestern state and one that was strongly rural. Schricker was the ideal man in every way to make the nominating speech. As Governor of the neighboring state of Indiana, he had a more intimate knowledge than Carvel of Stevenson's record. And although he was a firm believer in the Democratic Party, he had a wide appeal for Republicans and independents—a fact attested to by his record of having been the only person twice elected to the Indiana governorship since 1851.

But although these reasons seemed convincing to us, how could Carvel be dissuaded from placing Stevenson's name in nomination? In the first place, how and why had the situation come into being? What was to be lost by it? Could anything possibly be gained? These and many other questions needed answering.

For over five hours we discussed the pros and cons of every aspect of the problem. It was still hot, beastly hot. And we were still tired. Dave Garwin kept us going with coffee, milk, and rolls. The street lights had dimmed and street noises had pretty well quieted down. Yet we remained without a satisfactory course of action. How we grieved those early morning hours that *D* came before *I* in the alphabet!

At about five thirty in the morning we telephoned Joseph Solon, of our executive committee, to join us. We told him we needed a fresh mind to judge the mosaic we had been struggling with all night, that we had decided we should take any action necessary to make sure that the Carvel arrangement did not come to pass. We had analyzed the states ahead of Delaware on the roll-call, and while waiting for Solon to arrive, we tried unsuccessfully by phone calls to persuade some of their leaders to yield to Schricker.

Finally, when Solon came in, we reviewed briefly what had taken place and asked him for his opinion on how we could make Arvey understand that if the Carvel arrangement was not canceled, we would utilize every publicity medium possible to reveal the "deal" that had been "cooked up."

There were a few moments of silence. Solon walked over to the telephone, dialed a number, and said that he wanted to talk to Arvey. A brief pause, and Solon said: "Colonel, this is Joe Solon. I want Mr. Paul Butler of Indiana to tell you something." He then turned the phone over to Butler.

A fifteen-minute conversation ensued. Butler warned that Schricker was going to make the nomination or else Butler would raise the issue when the National Committee met. Arvey suggested a compromise: Carvel would speak first and then Schricker could deliver a second nominating speech.

Butler refused. Under great pressure from Butler, Arvey finally agreed that Carvel would yield to Schricker but that the nominating time would have to be shared equally, thus canceling any seconding speeches.

Butler then phoned Schricker and asked him to come over immediately, which the Governor did.

We then called Jonathan Daniels, who had a suite in the Hilton. He was still in bed, so we all went up to his rooms to see if he thought there was anything else we should do. I had by this time become over-cautious at making decisions, because we were pretty weary after the all-night session.

We also phoned Finnegan and Myers to tell them what had been happening. At first we were unable to reach them, owing to an early caucus they were attending with their delegation. When we finally reached them, we explained the arrangement that had been made. They were greatly relieved, for they, too, had heard the night before that Carvel was planning to place Stevenson's name in nomination. They themselves had been working most of those early morning hours trying to solve the problem.

They went onto the floor of the convention that morning and early afternoon to make sure that the agreement that Carvel would yield to Schricker was carried out. A blow-up on the floor over this matter, they knew, might cause a serious loss of votes and stall the draft. Finnegan's comment about the whole episode was most pertinent: "It's obvious what has happened. Everybody is on the bandwagon."

The Convention that fourth day was seething with anticipation. The day to place names in nomination had finally come. Would the speech for one of the candidates stampede the Convention? Would the efforts on behalf of the candidates be unavailing and then would the unbelievable occur—a draft of a genuinely reluctant man?

Before Stevenson's name was placed in nomination late Thursday afternoon, the Convention received the names of Senator Richard B. Russell, Senator Estes Kefauver, Senator Robert S. Kerr, Senator J. W. Fulbright, and Averell Harriman.[2]

When Delaware was reached on the roll-call of states, Carvel yielded to Schricker, who spoke for twelve and a half minutes, and ended his speech by saying:

In Governor Stevenson's own words the world looks to America for dignity, sanity, and confident leadership. His own humility, dignity, and capacity for confident leadership have, to a unique degree, excited the imagination, caught the fancy, and fired the hopes of the American people.

Ninety-two years ago, the nation called from the prairies

[2] Also placed in nomination were Governor G. Mennen Williams of Michigan, Senator Hubert Humphrey, Governor Paul Dever, Alben Barkley, and Oscar Ewing, Federal Security Administrator. Although Senator McMahon withdrew from the race for the nomination, Connecticut promised him its first-ballot vote anyway.

of Illinois the greatest of Illinois citizens, Abraham Lincoln. Lincoln too was reluctant. But there are times when a man is not permitted to say no.

I place before you the man we cannot permit to say no, Adlai E. Stevenson of Illinois.

Then the Convention gave itself over to a mass demonstration that it would not be denied Stevenson. "A tremendous cheer and mass of waving banners greeted the placing in nomination tonight of Gov. Adlai E. Stevenson of Illinois," Norton said in the *Baltimore Sun*. "It was easily the biggest, noisiest, longest and most spontaneous outburst of this long day of nominating speeches." And Felix Belair, Jr., pointed out in the *New York Times* that when Stevenson's name was offered to the Convention, "It was then that the convention really went wild."

That evening the newspapers reported that Stevenson had seen on television his old friend Schricker put his name in nomination. After the delegates stormed into the aisles—Carvel had to make his speech to a sea of "America Needs Stevenson" placards on the march—Stevenson issued this statement:

"I had hoped they would not nominate me, but I am deeply affected by this expression of confidence and goodwill."

Newsmen took this statement to mean that he would accept the draft nomination. And one reporter wrote: "Delegates generally accepted his statement as an oblique way of sending the long-awaited word." [3]

While the pro-Stevenson delegates were weaving

[3] *Chicago Sun-Times*, July 25.

through the Convention hall, Missouri caucused. The President's alternate, Thomas J. Gavin, announced, for the first time, that he had been instructed by President Truman to cast a vote for Stevenson. Quickly the word spread around the Convention that now the President was supporting the Illinois Governor.[4] And William S. White noted in the *New York Times:*

. . . As the convention struggled noisily forward through the fatigue of many hours the drive to select Mr. Stevenson, notwithstanding his reluctance, had become the first genuine draft movement since the Republican party demanded James A. Garfield in 1880.

[4] Carleton Kent had said in the *Chicago Sun-Times*, July 22: ". . . The Illinois Governor—once out of White House favor because he wouldn't jump at Mr. Truman's first offer of the nomination—was said to have slipped back into the good graces of the Chief Executive, largely because he appeared to be an odds-on winner."

CHAPTER XI

THE DRAFT CANNOT BE STOPPED: THURSDAY, FRIDAY, JULY 24–5

THE STEVENSON bandwagon "was rolling under a powerful head of steam" Thursday evening when a Convention row over the seating of Southern delegates not subscribing to the loyalty oath put a temporary halt to its forward movement. A battle royal occurred when Minnesota challenged the right of delegates who had not signed the loyalty oath to participate in the Convention. This battle had been brewing ever since the opening session on Monday.

At the session Monday evening a resolution was passed requiring all delegates to sign a loyalty pledge promising to use "all honorable" means to place the Convention's nominees under the Democratic column in their states. (Four years before, some Southern states had run their own "Dixiecrat" nominees on the Democratic ticket.) Prime movers behind the loyalty pledge were Franklin D. Roosevelt, Jr., the Harriman campaign manager; Michigan's Senator Blair Moody and Governor G. Mennen Williams; and Senator Hubert Humphrey of Minnesota.

Some Southern delegates protested that the pledge violated state laws or state party instructions. The next day a compromise interpretation, worked out by some party leaders, was announced by Representative Roosevelt. A proviso was added to the pledge saying that delegates should not be required to contravene state laws or state party instructions. Delegates still could not be seated, however, unless they undertook to do all in their power to ensure that the nominees of the Convention would appear as the Democratic nominees on the state ballots.

But Virginia, South Carolina, and Louisiana still refused to sign the loyalty pledge.

Minnesota's challenge on Thursday evening threw the Convention into a frenzy. "In no time at all the Democrats were fighting just like 1952 Republicans as America sat in front of its TV sets," *Life* remarked.

Maryland moved to seat Virginia even though its delegates had not signed the pledge. Leaders backing the Harriman and Kefauver candidacies fought the motion bitterly. Illinois voted 45 against to 15 for seating. When the roll-call reached Pennsylvania, that delegation by a strong majority voted to seat Virginia.

The Pennsylvania delegation reasoned that a Convention walkout by some delegations had to be prevented. The Democratic Party had more points of agreement than disagreement, and why, therefore, should it tear itself to pieces over this issue? [1] When Pennsylvania's vote, designed to hold the party together, was announced, there was considerable applause from both delegates and spectators.

When the last state had voted on this issue, Illinois announced that it was changing its votes to 52 to 8 in

[1] Finnegan and Myers to me, March 12, 1954.

favor of seating Virginia.[2] Several other delegations switched their votes and the final tally was 650½ for seating Virginia to 518 against.

The Kefauver-Harriman forces now tried to adjourn the Convention to regroup their forces and to prevent any balloting for the Presidential nominee that night. Senator Paul H. Douglas—who had announced his support of Kefauver after Stevenson's statement of April 16—moved adjournment. But adjournment was defeated by a roll-call vote.

The Convention was then thrown into a turmoil when the Kefauver-Harriman forces disrupted the Convention with parliamentary maneuvering and points of order. As Governor James F. Byrnes of South Carolina was being questioned about the loyalty pledge, a fire broke out on the Convention floor. It was quickly put out, and Byrnes humorously said: "I want to announce that I did not set the place on fire."

The laughter that followed Byrnes's remark eased the tension somewhat. The Convention then proceeded to seat South Carolina and Louisiana. At about two a.m. Friday morning, after thirteen and three-quarters hours in session, the Convention adjourned until eleven a.m.

Soon after the Convention adjourned, the Kefauver-

[2] Arvey has written that he and Joseph Gill, chairman of the Illinois delegation, were off the Convention floor when Illinois cast its vote. They hurried back and "It suddenly dawned on us what was happening. The strategy of the Kefauver backers and the Northern liberal bloc was to try to make impossible demands on the Southern delegates so that they would walk out of the Convention. If the Convention vote was thus cut down by the walkout of delegates who would never vote for Kefauver, then the Tennessee Senator would have a better chance of winning the nomination" (*Reporter*, November 24, 1953).

Harriman strategists held a much publicized "liberal-labor" caucus at the Congress Hotel. There was much talk of agreeing on one candidate to stop the Stevenson draft. Actually, as early as Tuesday, the 22nd, there had been meetings of the Harriman-Kefauver forces to discuss pooling their strength to halt the rush to the Illinois Governor.[3]

Many at the caucus charged that the switch by Illinois on seating Virginia was part of "a deal between Stevenson and the Dixiecrats." (Stevenson, as he told reporters, was not involved in the decision to switch the Illinois vote. And he did not receive the nomination on the third ballot as a result of votes by any of the Southern delegates who might have been forced out of the Convention.) [4]

The caucus was attended by Lerner, Ming, and I. J. Rosenbloom as observers from our committee. They ignored a warning from some of the caucus leaders not to attend. They pointed out that our committee had not been involved in the actions of the Illinois delegation. They also reminded the people present that Franklin D. Roosevelt, Jr., was incorrect in his charges at the caucus that Stevenson was not a progressively minded man. Senator Humphrey and Jack Kroll of the C.I.O., too, calmed the caucus and pointed to Stevenson's progressive record as Governor.

No decision was reached by this group on a candidate to stop the Illinois Governor.

Early that Friday morning rumors of another stop-Stevenson movement were flying around. Missouri

[3] See, for instance, the *New York Times*, July 23, 24.
[4] *Chicago Sun-Times*, July 25.

Senator Thomas C. Hennings, Jr., had placed Vice-President Barkley's name in nomination during the nominating roll-call the day before. The rumors asserted that some old-guard leaders hoped now to capitalize on the confusion created by the "liberal-labor" bloc and emerge out of it with the nomination for Mr. Barkley. (The rumors all agreed that Barkley was not participating in this movement.)

Even if the party then went down to defeat, the old guard would control the machinery of the National Committee for the next four years. (The Vice-President in the balloting on Friday did pick up strength, from 48½ votes on the first ballot to 78½ on the second. This, however, was not sufficient to indicate any real break in the Convention to stop Stevenson.)

Just before the Convention convened late Friday morning for balloting, Miss Pauline Frederick, of the American Broadcasting Company, came to our head-quarters and said she had been given the assignment of covering our activities that day.[5]

Mike Wallace of CBS, who had been making periodic checks the day before, came in almost on the heels of Miss Frederick. They both put the question: ". . . could they set up TV cameras on the 15th floor, just in case?" We told them we were trying to make facilities equal to all the press, radio, and television corps, but that the cameras would block up some of the hallway and create confusion. Finally arrange-

[5] Miss Frederick had been to see us frequently before this visit. After one interview she said on her network broadcast: "There is an entirely new language for political action being written on the fifteenth floor of the Hilton Hotel."

ments were made—not so satisfactorily as we or the television folks would have liked.

When the Convention met to start voting, the turmoil of the previous session was gone. Sam Rayburn, Speaker of the House of Representatives, and Chairman of the Convention, kept the Convention orderly as the balloting was conducted. Rayburn, as presiding officer, had been fair to all sides. He had allowed the various forces to have their say. Now, as the voting started, it was clear that he was determined to keep within the realm of decorum the history-making portion of the Convention.

One hour before the balloting began on Friday, the 25th, we estimated 272 votes for Stevenson on the first ballot. He received 273.

When the tally was announced to the Convention, Finnegan turned to Hubert Will on the Convention floor and said: "273 votes. You estimated 272. That's the trouble with dealing with you amateurs—you're not accurate!"

For the nomination 615½ votes were needed. On the first ballot Kefauver received 340; Harriman, 123½; Russell, 268; Barkley, 48½; Kerr, 65; Dever, 37½; Fulbright, 22; Humphrey, 26; besides the 272 for Stevenson. And there was a scattering of votes for a few others.[6]

On the second ballot Stevenson jumped from 273

[6] Stevenson's alternate in the Illinois delegation cast his vote for Harriman as instructed by Stevenson. For the voting state by state see *Official Report of the Proceedings of the Democratic National Convention* (Washington: Democratic National Committee; 1954), pp. 456, 484, 538.

to 324½; Kefauver increased to 362½; Harriman received 121, losing 2½ votes; Barkley went to 78½; Russell to 294; and forty-eight votes went to lesser candidates.

Although it may have seemed that the increase for Stevenson on the second ballot was not dramatic or large, we had not expected it to be. There were delegations committed to other candidates for two ballots which planned to shift to Stevenson on the third. Immediately at the close of the second ballot, Finnegan called me from the Convention to report that the arithmetic in our calculations was running as we had expected. "He will be nominated on the third ballot," Finnegan added.

At the close of the second ballot, it now being a quarter past six p.m., the Convention recessed for dinner. Shortly after New York had cast its vote on the second ballot, the delegation held a caucus. When the Convention reconvened, Paul Fitzpatrick, Democratic state chairman for New York, read a statement from Averell Harriman urging his supporters to vote for Stevenson.[7] Governor Dever of Massachusetts also announced his support of Stevenson and said that Stevenson would accept the nomination.[8]

[7] Harriman drafted this statement at about four p.m. During the dinner recess, President Truman sent a message to Harriman asking him to withdraw in favor of Stevenson, "but the President's influence was hardly necessary at this point." Paul T. David, Malcolm Moos, Ralph M. Goldman: *Presidential Nominating Politics in 1952: The National Story* (Baltimore: The Johns Hopkins Press; 1954), p. 154.

[8] Arvey says in the *Reporter*, November 24, 1953, that he called Stevenson after the first ballot. Dever was with him. Arvey asked Stevenson to tell Dever he would accept if nominated. When

The first state to swing on the final ballot was Arkansas with 20½ votes for Stevenson.[9] Massachusetts gave 25 to Stevenson. Michigan, which had given Kefauver 40 on each of the first two ballots, now gave all 40 to Stevenson.[1] Minnesota, which had given its 26 votes to Senator Humphrey on the first ballot, and 17 for Kefauver, 7½ for Stevenson, and 1½ for Harriman on the second, gave 13 to Stevenson on the third. New York, which had had only 6½ Stevenson votes on the previous ballots, now registered 86½ for him. Pennsylvania, which had cast 36 votes for Stevenson on the first ballot and 40 on the second, now gave him its entire 70. With the Pennsylvania vote, it was now clear that Stevenson would have the nomination on this third ballot.

While the balloting was taking place in the International Amphitheatre at the stock yards on Chicago's southwest side, miles away on the near north side there was frenzied activity. The quiet of fashionable Astor Street—where Stevenson was staying as the guest of William McCormick Blair, Jr.—was disrupted by the activities of reporters, photographers, television cameramen, and sound trucks. Thirty photographers and reporters waited outside the three-story brick house. Linemen strung wires through the walled garden to the street, where six pay-station telephone booths were set up for the reporters.

Arvey assured Stevenson that the Convention couldn't agree on anyone else, Stevenson told Dever he would accept.

[9] On the first ballot Arkansas had given its votes to Senator Fulbright; on the second, 18 for Russell, 1½ for Kefauver, 1½ for Stevenson.

[1] Michigan cast its original vote on the first ballot for Governor Williams, but changed to Kefauver at the conclusion of the roll-call.

"This is the most excitement we've had on this street for years," remarked a uniformed nurse as she walked a child past the house.

Except for breakfast with Averell Harriman that morning at the apartment where Mr. and Mrs. Ernest Ives—the Governor's sister and brother-in-law—were staying, Stevenson remained secluded at "Blair House."

Although Stevenson was a delegate, he had not returned to the Convention after his speech of welcome. On Friday he was so cautious about staying out of Convention activities, and doing nothing that would indicate he was promoting his own chances that he even refused an invitation from McKinney to have dinner with President Truman, who had flown to Chicago that afternoon.

When it became clear that Stevenson would receive the nomination on the third ballot, the two co-chairmen of the Draft Committee made these statements to the TV audience:

Leo A. Lerner said:

This nomination was made without any attempt on the part of Governor Stevenson to enlist the support of party bosses or to harness the party machine. Governor Stevenson is the choice of a free convention and he can unify both the party and the country. His candidacy was promoted by a popular "Draft Stevenson" movement consisting entirely of independent businessmen, citizens, professional people, representatives of organized labor, and other Americans who want good government. At this time, I want to offer hearty thanks to the hundreds of volunteers, without whose eager help the "Draft Stevenson" movement could not have succeeded.

As the other co-chairman, I said:

We are proud and grateful that we were instrumental through voluntary inspiration to give the nation and the world the new Wilson in the person of Governor Adlai E. Stevenson.

I personally feel a great calm and a sense of history; at this moment in American history, we need reason and deliberation to solve our problems. We need a sense of dignity and wisdom if we are to survive as a free people. With Governor Stevenson this nation can move forward to solve our problems intelligently and rationally.

The service of our volunteer staff has been a miracle of enthusiasm. Few political movements in history have seen such spontaneous success. We volunteers will carry on.

Meanwhile on the Convention floor, with the nomination over just after midnight, the stage was set for Stevenson's acceptance speech; but it took a long time for the curtain to go up. Word went around the Convention hall that President Truman would address the delegates and present the nominee. Senator Russell and Senator Kefauver spoke. Weary minutes passed. The lights beat down through a stale haze of cigarette and cigar smoke. The floor was littered with torn papers.

The giant organ boomed out "Don't Let 'Em Take It Away," over and over again. Then it swung into every state song that anybody had ever heard. The crowd sang and cheered, but as the hour dragged past one o'clock in the morning, throats were husky and eyes glazed. Exhaustion battled with anticipation. The delegates wanted to see the man they had nominated and then go out and get a little sleep.

At last the President strode onto the rostrum, waving jauntily to the audience. He launched into a fighting speech, strong with the echoes of the 1948 whistle-stop campaign. As he finished, he introduced Stevenson, and the crowd, tired, strained, and restless as they were, sat forward to listen to a new kind of acceptance speech from a new kind of candidate.

A sense of drama gripped that tired throng as Stevenson began to talk. People in the press box grabbed the advance text of the speech, absorbed it greedily, then sat back to listen to the words they had read.

President Truman's speech furnished a springboard for a leap from the political past into the future. The Stevenson speech took the leap with dazzling grace in such paragraphs as these:

I hope and pray that we Democrats, win or lose, can campaign not as a crusade to exterminate the opposing party, as our opponents seem to prefer, but as a great opportunity to educate and elevate a people whose destiny is leadership, not alone of a rich and prosperous, contented country as in the past, but of a world in ferment.

And, my friends, even more important than winning the election is governing the nation. That is the test of a political party—the acid, final test. When the tumult and the shouting die, when the bands are gone and the lights are dimmed, there is the stark reality of responsibility in an hour of history haunted with those gaunt, grim specters of strife, dissension and ruthless, inscrutable and hostile power abroad.

The ordeal of the Twentieth Century—the bloodiest, most turbulent era of the Christian age—is far from over. Sacrifice, patience, understanding and implacable purpose may be our lot for years to come.

Let's face it. Let's talk sense to the American people. Let's tell them the truth, that there are no gains without pains, that we are now on the eve of great decisions, not easy decisions, like resistance when you're attacked, but a long, patient, costly struggle which alone can assure triumph over the great enemies of man—war, poverty and tyranny—and the assaults upon human dignity which are the most grievous consequences of each.

CHAPTER XII

WHO DRAFTED ADLAI STEVENSON?

THAT HE was drafted cannot be gainsaid.

It was the first draft since Hughes, and the only time in the modern history of the Democratic Party when a man who didn't want the nomination received it. Deadlocks like the one in 1924 had occurred and individuals had been drafted. But these individuals had not asked the delegates not to vote for them nor had they thrown every obstacle—except a Sherman-like statement—in the path of those trying to draft them.

Adlai Stevenson really did sit back. He did not plan what happened. He made no deals, no commitments, and no gestures of encouragement. The office sought the man—historically, the essence of a draft, the reason why drafts have the connotation of political purity.

Mayor David L. Lawrence has written:

I have been in politics all my life. My father and grandfather before me were also in politics. I have heard of many so-called drafts, but the drafting of Stevenson was the only completely genuine draft of which I have ever known. . . .[1]

The press comment at the close of the Convention laid stress on the authentic nature of the draft. "This

[1] Letter to me, April 15, 1954.

was a genuine draft of a genuinely reluctant candidate," L. C. Eklund said in the *Milwaukee Journal* on July 27. "The president himself was the first to admit this at the tumultuous early morning convention session Saturday when he said that Stevenson was nominated because 'he would not make deals with anybody.' That was not political hokum."

Irving Dilliard editorialized in the *St. Louis Post-Dispatch* on July 26:

The ideal in American public life is to have the office seek the man. At the Democratic National Convention in Chicago, the nomination for the presidency has sought out and found a man.

. . . Because the nomination sought him, Adlai Stevenson can regard himself as a free agent, beholden to no group or groups within the party or to any collection of individuals or leader of any kind. . . .

Stevenson did not "connive" to secure the nomination. The draft astounded those who had said that it could not succeed unless he let party leaders know he wanted it. Many of these leaders were plaintive with him, then bewildered when he rejected all overtures.

Walter Lippmann wrote on July 24:

. . . There is no doubt, I think, that from the beginning Stevenson has seen the reality of the situation with extraordinary objectivity and penetration. He has not been coy. He has been wise in realizing what after 20 years in office it would mean to take over the leadership of the Democratic party.

It could be done only under conditions which, if not unique in politics, are very rare indeed. The new leadership had to draw its strength from the mass of the party, not from the outgoing president. There was no value in the kind of nomination for which Vice President Barkley was, so cynically and so briefly, considered.

The new leadership had to be drafted. It could not be appointed from the White House. A draft, as everyone knows, is almost never genuine. In the case of Stevenson, if he is nominated, there will have been a genuine draft. He will have been drafted because the party needs the man more than he desired the office. To have known this is the mark of wisdom. To have adhered to it is the mark of great public virtue.

If Stevenson is nominated under these conditions, he can, therefore, assume the leadership entirely in his own right, quite uncommitted to any faction.

The actual conditions that developed at the Convention from July 16 to the nomination completely nullified previous plans and assumptions developed by many leaders and candidates. The new factors introduced by Stevenson's attitude toward the nomination and by the political action of our committee could not be handled by any traditional formula.

The spontaneous upsurge for Stevenson forms a fascinating chapter in American politics. The upsurge continued from January 1952 through to his nomination in spite of discouraging statements from him and lulls and low points that demonstrate that the draft was not inevitable; and in spite of lack of support from many key party leaders who had earlier wanted him to run. They pessimistically turned to other possibilities as the Convention approached.

The Democratic Convention was the first uncontrolled Convention of the party since 1932. No one knew what the Convention would do. An increasing number of the delegates relished their freedom not to have to accept dictation in the exercise of their franchise. These delegates honestly and fervently wanted Stevenson. They drafted the Illinois Governor as being, in their minds, the most formidable man the Democrats had.

In the *New York Times* the day after Stevenson's speech of welcome to the Convention, the late Anne O'Hare McCormick concluded:

> . . . In one day, in fact, all the confused and un-channeled currents seemed to converge on the shrinking figure of Governor Adlai Stevenson as the one and only, the almost automatic choice of the convention. Nothing but action by the President could alter the picture, and the general feeling here is that even that would now be too late.

Governor Stevenson's position was not established by a vote. It is hard to determine just how, in a day in which nothing decisive happened except the defeat of the Southern states on the pledge of loyalty to the party, everybody's race suddenly narrowed down to put the laggard in the lead. It was not Mr. Stevenson's welcoming speech, freshminted and sparkling as it was after the torrents of stale oratory we have heard in the past fortnight. The stampede of welcome for him came before he opened his mouth. As the cheers turned into cries of "We want Stevenson!" the clamor sounded as if the delegates, whose allegiance was uneasily divided among many candidates, none of whom was sure to win, all at once found what they were looking for—someone on whom they might be united, someone who had a chance of beating Eisenhower. It was as if the convention acted on an unplanned, instinctive impulse of its own. The Democratic party organization had as little to do with it as the Republican party organization had to do with the demand for Eisenhower. In both parties we are witnessing a crumbling of the old machinery of power. In one case it is worn out from functioning too long, in the other it is rusty from disuse. . . .

The Stevenson qualities which attracted the enthusiastic support of our committee were also well known to the pro-Stevenson delegates: his single term as Governor of Illinois had revealed that he was a warm, intelligent, vigorous leader; he was liberal in spirit and moderate in method; he had raised political debate to a new high in Illinois; and he was a proved vote-getter.

His speech of welcome to the Convention demonstrated to the delegates not committed to drafting him what a formidable, intelligent, literate leader he was.[2]

Writing during the Convention, Raymond A. McConnell, Jr., editor of the Lincoln [Nebraska] *State Journal*, analyzed the appeal of Stevenson in terms of the public being deathly sick of pride, pomp, cant, and self-seeking. The people, he wrote, turn "to an Eisenhower, or a Stevenson, not because these men profess to know more than others but because in the

[2] Arthur Krock said in the *New York Times* on September 15, 1952: "His two speeches at the Chicago convention . . . restored the level of political oratory in this country to that which Woodrow Wilson occupied."

humility of true greatness they confess to their own shortcomings. . . ." [3]

Stevenson's own qualities, then, and his record as Governor of Illinois were immensely significant factors in the Stevenson draft.

Another significant factor was his appeal as a leader who could unite the party. He was not a leader of a faction of the party.[4] Each of the major parties con-

[3] *Chicago Daily News*, July 23.

[4] Stevenson has explained his view of the nature of the Democratic Party this way: ". . . I can say that I am a Democrat because I believe that the Democratic Party has been faithful to the people as a whole, and to the root concept of equal rights for all and special privileges for none. And I believe that over its long history, the Democratic Party has been much more alert and adaptable to our needs, be they defenses against economic misfortune, or the realities of the uneasy world about us. I believe that properly informed, continuously and accurately informed, the people will know best in the long run, better than any one of us or any group of us, better than Alexander Hamilton's 'rich and well born' or Karl Marx's 'proletariat.'

"The Democratic Party has survived the Federalists, the Whigs and all manner of less enduring parties because, by and large, it has clung to the broad concept of a people's party. I hope it will not become just a labor party, or a farmer's party, or a minorities party, or a small-business party, or reflect predominantly the views and economic interest of any group in our society. When it does, it will fail in its historic mission as a means to an end—as a mechanism for the expression of general opinion and for the development of public policy for the attainment of the basic objective of a truly democratic society—the always imperfect but ever-expanding well-being and freedom of all the people.

"These are broad strokes of the philosophic brush and there is much more I could say about the Democratic Party, critical as well as approving, for I make no pretenses about the wisdom, virtue, or infallibility of Democrats. Indeed, I think self-examination and criticism are the great and not-so-secret weapons of democracy. And criticism and nonconformity seem to come naturally to us Democrats who represent such diversity and have no taste for the irons of rigid uniformity and discipline. As Marse Henry Watterson said, 'Things have come to a pretty pass when a man can't cudgel his own jackass.' " *Major Campaign Speeches of Adlai E. Stevenson*, p. xiv.

tains a diverse range of leaders and groups. The contending factions struggle within the party framework for dominance or, if not for dominance, for a share of control and reward.

The basic strength for Stevenson was in the local and state units of the party, which wanted a candidate who could unify the party for victory. Archibald Alexander has said: "I am convinced that the vast majority of those who supported Stevenson during the critical period were small and unimportant individuals, from 20 or more states, and that it was only after the strength of this number became apparent that many of the seasoned politicians felt it safe to join the Stevenson cause. Their worst fear was always of backing a loser."

Candidates for office—particularly candidates for the Senate and the House of Representatives—who wanted to win, and who knew that Stevenson at the head of the ticket would be a tremendous asset in their own campaigns, were a particularly potent force in the draft.

And the National Committee Stevenson For President played a vital role in the Stevenson draft. Through our stimulation of newspaper, radio, and TV comment about Stevenson, we helped establish confidence in the minds of many party leaders and Convention delegates that a draft could and would be successful. Public opinion naturally affects delegates at a convention. And the press, radio, and TV help in turn to formulate that public opinion.

We furnished a headquarters where leaderless, uncontrolled delegates who wanted Stevenson could rally their forces and co-operate with pro-Stevenson delegates from other states. And our committee, with its enthusiasm for Stevenson, contributed to the growing faith and confidence that he was the only man for the nomination.

We also performed the significant function of calling the leaders of Pennsylvania, Indiana, New Jersey, and Kansas together in the very first instance. With them we planned the organization of the draft machinery. Beginning Tuesday, July 22, the main activities of the draft naturally centered around the floor leader, Francis Myers.

When Stevenson paid his first visit to our headquarters, on the afternoon of July 26, hours after his nomination, he was asked by the swarm of reporters with him what he thought of us. He replied:

"I was running backwards fine until I tripped over Johnson and Lerner."

When a *Chicago Tribune* reporter said to Stevenson: "I thought you said you wouldn't ever come here," the Governor, with a sparkle in his eyes, remarked:

"I came up to rebuke them for doing such a nonprofessional job in such a professional way."

Just after Stevenson received the nomination, Malvina Lindsay said in the *Washington Post*:

His gift of being articulate may have played no small part in the phenomenal draft by which he has been made, against his desire, his party's candidate for President. For most of the credit for keeping the Stevenson boom going, after the Governor had publicly backed away from efforts of the White House and of party leaders to get behind him, goes to a little group of practical political scientists headed by Prof. Walter Johnson of the history department of the University of Chicago. . . .

And a correspondent for *Time,* in an unpublished background piece on the draft, wrote:

. . . Just about every shred of specific evidence available in Chicago this week supports the claim of Stevenson intimates and backers that the draft movement was absolutely what it appeared to be—a spontaneous, highly unorganized ground swell which developed and blossomed without a single boost and with only utterly tacit encouragement from the draftee himself.

This reporter then added that he had searched for the "dark threads of Machiavellian plot and could not find so much as a dropped stitch. How then did machinery of the draft Stevenson movement develop at the Convention? The beginning point is," he wrote, "the National Committee Stevenson For President. . . ."

Perhaps the draft of Stevenson would have occurred even if we had not been in existence. But, then again, it might not have.

Perhaps it is impossible to appraise the contribution of our committee. It is quite clear that we could not have functioned successfully if there had not already been pro-Stevenson sentiment in some delegations.

But assuming that a draft might have occurred without us, it is likely that Stevenson's name would not have been placed in nomination on the first rollcall. It might have come about only when a party beset by too many candidates reached a deadlock after prolonged balloting. By such a time, it is quite possible that the bitterness created among the factions would have resulted in a badly divided party.

Such a draft, too, would probably have come about as the result of the efforts of a few party leaders striving to prevent chaos. It would not have represented the broad upsurge of the successful draft with its broadly based combination of some party leaders, rank and file delegates, and the Citizen's Committee.

The Draft Stevenson Committee lonesomely persisted until sentiment crystallized. When this occurred—and the meeting called by the Kansas delegation on Saturday the 19th failed to evolve any structure for the draft—we took the responsibility of putting together the machinery of the draft.

Then, on the 20th and 21st of July we initiated the organization of the draft machinery. At this point the draft was by no means an assured thing. Alexander has written: ". . . there were several times in the three or four days immediately before the convention and during the first two or three days during the convention when the failure of no more than one or two people to pursue the effort to nominate Stevenson would have resulted in the nomination of someone else."

The publicity on Tuesday the 22nd about the steps taken, Stevenson's speech of welcome delivered on the 21st, and Barkley's withdrawal that night, all combined to create a fast-moving Stevenson bandwagon by Tuesday afternoon, the 22nd.

Beginning on Tuesday, many party leaders quickly jumped aboard a bandwagon that was rolling so well that they had no alternative unless they wanted to see it pass them by.

The Alsops wrote in their syndicated column for August 3:

> . . . The plain fact is that Mr. Truman and the "bosses" who are supposed to have maneuvered the Stevenson draft were themselves caught flat-footed when it became clear that the convention wanted Stevenson and nobody else.
>
> In effect, the professionals simply rushed to the head of the Stevenson parade which was already forming, and began frantically waving their banners. . . .

Leaders who had pessimistically turned away from him in the weeks before the Convention, were not again for him until after July 22. Arvey, too, by early July had abandoned hope that Stevenson could be drafted, though he regularly stated that he thought Stevenson would accept if nominated.

When Alexander phoned Arvey early in July, the Illinois National Committeeman told him he could not discuss the Stevenson candidacy at all in view of the Governor's request that he do nothing to promote a Stevenson draft. After Alexander had arrived in Chicago, he was unable to reach Arvey and did not hear from him until after the nomination.

Arvey was not a factor in the organizing of the Draft Stevenson machinery. There is no doubt, however, that his statement in the Illinois caucus on July 20 that although his delegation wouldn't place Stevenson's name in nomination, they reserved the right to vote as they saw fit, gave support to the draft sentiment. But the Illinois delegation decided at that point not to vote for Stevenson on the first ballot.

The delegation itself became restive over this decision and became concerned that it was "looking silly." By late Tuesday, July 22, the Illinois delegation decided to cast its Stevenson votes on the first ballot. It did not lead the draft bandwagon; it merely climbed aboard when the draft was well on its way. And it had to share the space on the wagon with those who had filled the vacuum—a vacuum that might not otherwise have been filled.

The leaders from Pennsylvania, Indiana, New Jersey, and Kansas working to secure delegate votes— with the aid of our committee—remained the vital force in the Stevenson draft through the third ballot. But by the third day of the Convention others were trying to emerge as the leaders of the draft. The incident involving Governor Carvel's desire to place Stevenson in nomination is one such example.

The American Political Science Association's five-volume study of *Presidential Nominating Politics in 1952: The National Story,* under the direction of Paul T. David, interprets the Carvel episode in the following way:

Perhaps it can be concluded from all this that the Stevenson nomination would have been arranged even if the Draft Stevenson committee had not taken it upon itself to make the necessary arrangements. At the same time, however, the question remains as to whether a draft arranged by the convention management would not have taken on a coloration that might have prevented the reluctant candidate from accepting. . . . At any rate, it

seems fair to conclude that the activities of the Draft
Stevenson committee did much to make the Stevenson
nomination a genuine draft, however much stage management was also being undertaken by other kingmakers.[5]

In the context of the time, the Democratic Party
needed a candidate to whom no "deals," "claims," or
"factions" could be attached. These are the normal
charges of the opposition in a political campaign.
Furthermore, Republican Party strategy had already
manifested just that: "time for a change," "left-wing
control," "machine-boss control," and many others.

The natural rebuttal was, of course, an honest choice
without any strings or promises. And for any one
political faction within the whole of the Democratic
Party to have been the dominant "influence," even
by inference, would have impaired the value of going
to the country with complete candor.

Besides, the party within itself had been working for
two years toward compromising the vast distance
between factions. For any one element to emerge
dominant involved the danger of party suicide.

Actually, many party leaders were caught flat-footed
when the Convention demonstrated that it wanted
Stevenson and no one else. Then they rushed to get
on the bandwagon—a bandwagon that was rolling
well. That the new additions contributed to the re-
sulting nomination there is no question. That they
"master-minded" it is untrue.

That labor leaders "master-minded" the draft is
also incorrect. After the ten C.I.O. and A.F.L. leaders

[5] Page 138.

helped end the candidacy of Vice-President Barkley, labor was split between Harriman and Kefauver, with Stevenson sentiment growing among some of the labor delegates. David Dubinsky, president of the International Ladies Garment Workers Union and Vice-Chairman of the Liberal Party, and Alex Rose of the United Hatters, Cap and Millinery Workers Union, were the only two leading labor figures who came out for Stevenson early in the Convention.

The question of whom labor should support was settled by the Stevenson boom. "Labor's problem then," *Newsweek* pointed out on August 4, "was to get on the Stevenson bandwagon as quickly as possible. The reason: it wanted to appear responsible for pushing the governor across."

It must be remembered, of course, that many party leaders and many labor leaders had favored Stevenson in the spring of 1952. When he proved adamant in his refusal to be a candidate, they committed themselves to other candidates. Then, after the draft got under way at the Convention, many of them returned to their support of Stevenson after honoring commitments to support others on the first and second ballots.

Summing up the significance of Stevenson's nomination, Alistair Cooke wrote:

. . . So Stevenson emerged in triumph and in singularly happy independence. He owes nothing to the South, nothing to the Northern liberals. He is his own man. And in the last hour, after a jolly but perfunctorily received introduction by the President, he showed them what a formidable manner of man that is. His famous decorum hardened into magnanimity, his wit into principle, his integrity stayed the same. . . .

Out of this throbbing circus, its blowsy barkers and its super-subtle medicine men, emerged a humble and civilized man. It should not be forgotten that he was the choice of the gaping rustics and the family men who did not much fancy the glamour of the sideshows and the ringmasters and the miracle healers.[6]

Perhaps this account of how Stevenson was nominated can best be summed up, and closed, by a statement of a twelve-year-old boy.

After the excitement, action, and work of the Convention had ended, CBS commentators Edward R. Murrow, Eric Sevareid, and Walter Cronkite were doing their final broadcast and roundup. Each was expressing observations and interpretations. The matter of an uncontrolled Convention, the draft movement, the delegates making a full and free choice, the political action of the Draft Committee, the arithmetic of votes—all these came in for review.

Finally Mr. Sevareid told of bringing his twelve-year-old son, Peter, to the Convention hall several evenings earlier. Peter looked around the great hall, at the delegates, the spectators, the working press, and officials, the clouds of smoke fogging the lights.

And then Peter said to his father: "I guess this is the smoke-filled room they talk about."

[6] *Manchester Guardian,* July 28.

ACKNOWLEDGMENTS

MANY INDIVIDUALS furnished me with useful suggestions
and information for this book.

I am particularly indebted to the late Stuart Haydon
for his invaluable assistance.

David L. Cohn, another old friend and a talented writer,
shared with me his wisdom as an interpreter of American
life.

And to Alfred A. Knopf my thanks for the benefit of
his keen editorial insight.

My associates on the National Committee Stevenson
for President—Leo A. Lerner, Hubert Will, George Overton, Gwen Glasser, Marshall Holleb, W. R. Ming, Jr.,
Florence Medow, Joseph Solon, Maurice Rosenfield, Paul
Berger, and Richard Meyer—were most helpful.

Useful suggestions on background information came
from Barry Bingham, Louis A. Kohn, and Robert Notti.

A number of delegates who worked at the Convention
with the Draft Committee made most useful suggestions,
particularly James A. Finnegan, Francis J. Myers, David
Lawrence, Archibald Alexander, Henry F. Schricker, Paul
Butler, and Jonathan Daniels.

I am grateful to Random House and the Johns Hopkins
University Press for permission to quote from books published by them, and to Time Inc., and the *Reporter,* and
to the newspapers which have permitted me to quote
from material that appeared in their publications.

A portion of the material in this book was presented

as lectures on the Walgreen Foundation at the University of Chicago. I am indebted to Professor Jerome Kerwin, Secretary of the Walgreen Foundation, for his assistance.

My thanks to Alma Lach, who typed the manuscript, should be recorded, too.

INDEX

Abel, Elie, 61
Agricultural Adjustment Administration, 13
Alabama, 110
Alexander, Archibald, 72, 80–2, 86, 101, 110, 111, 113, 121, 122, 128, 162, 165, 166
Alexander, Lou, 122, 123
Alsop, Joseph, 23, 28, 60, 67, 78, 80, 109, 127, 128, 166
Alsop, Stewart, 23, 28, 60, 67, 78, 80, 109, 127, 128, 166
Altgeld, John Peter, 105
American Broadcasting Company, 148
American Federation of Labor, 124, 168
Americans for Democratic Action, 21, 33
American Political Science Association, 167
American Veterans Committee, 49
Anderson, Rev. Harrison R., 98–9
Anderson, Kenneth, 77, 85, 86, 101, 110, 122
Anderson, Mary S., 21, 48
Arkansas, 43, 113, 151
Arvey, Jacob, 15, 32–3, 34–5, 37, 51–3, 60–1, 63, 65, 68, 80, 89, 99, 112, 127, 131, 132, 137–40, 146, 150, 151, 166
Asia, 15
Associated Press, 125
Atlantic Monthly, 28

Bailey, John M., 110
Baltimore News-Post, 115

Baltimore Sun, 63, 65, 68, 85, 102, 113, 135, 142
Barkley, Alben, 45, 60, 77, 80, 89, 123–8, 129, 134, 141, 148, 149, 150, 158, 165, 169
Barr, Joseph, 98
Baxter, R. W., 110
Belair, Felix, Jr., 142
Belgium, 13
Berger, Paul H., 21, 48
Bernhard, Edgar, 21
Biddle, Francis, 86
Biffle, Leslie, 127
Bingham, Barry, 19
Blaine, James G., 70
Blair, William McCormick, Jr., 19, 151
Blair House, 18
Blatt, Genevieve, 98
Bloom, Sol, 14
Bloomington, 7, 12
Bloomington Pantagraph, 13
Boston Globe, 45, 115, 116
Brandt, Raymond P., 63, 66, 116
Bricker, John William, 121
Bromfield, Louis, 134
Brunner, George, 110
Brunswick, Joseph, 123
Bryan, William Jennings, 7, 71
Bulkley, Robert J., 110
Burkholder, Dan, 34
Butler, Paul M., 101, 110, 136–7, 139–40
Byrnes, James F., 14, 146

California, 35, 36, 110, 130
Carlebach, William D., 84, 110
Carvel, Elbert N., 129, 137–40, 141, 142, 167

Chadwell, Constance, 48
Changes, William G., Jr., 111
Charles Evans Hughes (Pusey), 83
Chicago Daily News, 28, 50, 129, 131, 161
Chicago Herald-American, 131
Chicago Sun-Times, 21, 22, 36, 61, 63, 67–8, 78, 115, 142, 143, 147
Chicago Tribune, 163
Childs, Marquis, 24, 61
Christian Science Monitor, 24, 63, 116, 134
Clark, F. Davis, 110
Clark, James P., 98
Clay, Henry, 71
Clay, John, 123
Cleveland, Charles B., 131
Cleveland, Grover, 7
Cleveland Plain Dealer, 115
Cohen, Milton, 123
Collier's, 28
Colorado, 110
Columbia Broadcasting System, 125, 148, 170
Communism, 106
Congress of Industrial Organizations, 85, 124, 147, 168
Connally, Tom, 14
Connecticut, 110, 141
Considine, Robert, 72
Cooke, Alistair, 169
Craig, May, 27
Cronkite, Walter, 170

Dallas, 35
Daniels, Jonathan, 75, 110, 140
David, Paul T., 150, 167
Delaware, 129, 137, 139, 141
Democratic National Committee, 42, 53–4, 60, 76, 85, 89, 92, 110, 121, 122, 128, 136, 140, 148, 149, 157
Democratic Party, 15, 20, 38–41, 49, 56, 62, 72, 76, 77, 78,

Democratic Party (*continued*) 81, 83, 84, 90, 93, 100, 103, 106–8, 121, 124, 138, 145, 154, 156, 160, 161, 168
Denton, Winfield K., 101
Dever, Paul A., 68, 80, 81, 141, 149, 150, 151
De Voto, Bernard, 24
Dewey, Thomas E., 116
Dilliard, Irving, 157
DiSalle, Michael, 81, 121
Douglas, Emily Taft, 50
Douglas, Paul H., 50, 146
Draft Stevenson Committee, 26, 45, 47, 51, 66, 79, 85, 99, 101, 112, 113, 121, 123, 152, 165, 166, 167–8, 170; *see also* National Committee Stevenson for President
Drummond, Roscoe, 116, 134
Dubinsky, David, 169
Dunne, Edward F., 105

Edmunds, George F., 70
Eiger, Richard N., 21, 48
Eiger, Mrs. Richard N., 48
Eisenhower, Dwight D., 12, 36, 75, 78, 131, 159
Eklund, L. C., 157
England, 13
Epps, David, 110
Europe, 11
Ewing, Ann, 48, 136
Ewing, Oscar, 141

Farley, James A., 129–30
Federal Alcohol Control Administration, 13
Fell, Jesse, 7, 15
Finnegan, James A., 77, 86, 87, 88–9, 91–3, 95, 98, 100, 102, 110, 112, 113, 121, 122, 128, 140, 141, 145, 149, 150
Fitzpatrick, Paul, 150
Flanagan, Maureen, 136
Fleeson, Doris, 103, 130

Fleming, Dewey, 85
Folliard, Edward T., 63
Foster, William, 121
Fort Worth Star-Telegram, 23
Frain, Andrew, 117, 122
France, 13
Frederick, Pauline, 148
Freidin, Seymour, 117
Fulbright, J. W., 113, 141, 149,
    151

Garfield, James A., 69–70, 82,
    143
Garwin, David, 46, 48, 139
Garwin, Jean, 48
Gavin, Thomas J., 143
Gill, Joseph L., 131–2, 134, 146
Gilstrap, Max K., 63
Glasser, Gwen, 21, 33, 34
Gluck, Joseph, 110
Goldman, Ralph M., 150
Goldmark, John, 111
Granger, Walter, 121
Grant, Ulysses S., 70
Grossberg, Herbert, 123

Hamilton, Alexander, 161
Hancock, Winfield S., 70
Harding, Warren G., 9
Harper's Magazine, 24
Harriman, Averell, 20, 21, 31–3,
    59, 75, 125, 128, 135, 141,
    144, 145, 146, 147, 149, 150,
    151, 152, 169
Harvard University, 58
Hawaii, 85
Hawkins, Lex, 110
Haydon, Stuart, 48, 50, 51, 54,
    62, 89, 137
Hayes, John A., 121
Hennings, Thomas C., Jr., 148
Hirsh, Morris H., 123
Hitchcock, Frank, 83
Hoar, George F., 70
Hogan, M. P., 110

Holleb, Marshall, 21, 48, 49,
    89, 122
Horner, Henry, 105
House of Representatives, 64,
    84, 149, 162
Hoyt, Calvin, 123
Hughes, Charles Evans, 82–3,
    156
Humphrey, Hubert, 141, 144,
    147, 149, 151
Hunt, Robert, 123
Hutton, Frank R., 84, 110
Hyde Park Herald (Chicago),
    45

Idaho, 110
Illinois Committee Stevenson
    For President, 19, 20, 22, 28;
    see also Draft Stevenson Com-
    mittee; *also* National Com-
    mittee Stevenson for President
Illinois Delegation, 134, 145,
    147, 149, 166–7
Illinois Legislature, 7–8
Independent Voters of Illinois,
    20–2
India, 15
Indiana, 64, 67, 68, 86, 100,
    101, 110, 123, 132, 134, 136,
    137, 138, 163, 167
Indianapolis, 64
International Ladies Garment
    Workers Union, 169
Iowa, 110
Italy, 11, 13, 15
Ives, Ernest, 152
Ives, Mrs. Ernest, 152

Johanson, Homer, 123
Johnson, Walter, 21, 57, 101,
    110, 163, 164

Kalven, Harry, Jr., 132
Kansas, 77, 85, 86, 87, 100, 110,
    122, 123, 132, 163, 165, 167
Karelsen, Frank E., Jr., 77

Keenan, Joseph, 124
Kefauver, Estes, 20, 21, 27, 28, 33, 45, 59, 75, 89, 102, 110, 125, 128, 130, 134, 136, 141, 145, 146, 147, 149, 150, 151, 153, 169
Kelley, Robert, 62
Kennedy, John, 117, 121
Kent, Carleton, 143
Kerr, Robert S., 20, 28, 45, 59, 141
Key West, 19
Kieran, John, 72
Klein, Robert, 22, 48
Knapp, Robert, 21
Knox, Frank, 13
Korea, 19
Krensky, Mary Jane, 48
Krock, Arthur, 24, 30, 160
Kroll, Jack, 124, 147

Lake Success, 14
Lane, John, 110
Larsen, Gilbert, 110
Lawler, Michael, 98
Lawrence, David, 78
Lawrence, David L., 81, 92, 98, 100, 102, 103, 113, 127–8, 129, 156
Leach, Paul R., 129
Leban, Howard, 118
Leban, John L., 118
Lerner, Leo A., 21, 47, 49, 53, 101, 110, 130, 147, 152, 163
Liberal Party, 169
Life, 28, 62, 145
Lincoln, Abraham, 7, 10, 12, 71, 142
Lindsay, Malvina, 163
Lindsay, Vachel, 105
Lippmann, Walter, 77–8, 157
London, 14
Long, Oren E., 85
Look, 28
Lord, Thorn, 110
Lord, Mrs. Thorn, 77, 110

Louisiana, 145, 146
Louisville, Ky., 19
Louisville Courier-Journal, 19, 49, 61, 65
Lucas, Scott, 37
Lukiewski, Helen, 121

Madigan, John, 131
Maine, 27, 70, 110
Major Campaign Speeches of Adlai E. Stevenson, 6, 37, 161
Mallin, Milton, 123
Manchester Guardian, 170
Marx, Karl, 161
Maryland, 135, 145
Massachusetts, 50, 68, 70, 80, 81, 117, 150, 151
Massey, Frank, 101
McCarthy, Joseph, 23
"McCarthyism," 10
McConnell, Raymond A., Jr., 160
McCormick, Anne O'Hare, 159
McKelway, B. M., 45, 63
McKendree College, 11
McKinney, Frank, 89, 128, 129, 152
McLaughlin, Joseph, 121, 136
McMahon, Brien, 135, 141
Medow, Florence, 34, 48
Merriam, Robert E., 50
Metzenbaum, Howard M., 110
Meyer, Richard A., 21
Michigan, 68, 141, 144, 151
Middle East, 15
Milwaukee Journal, 44, 100, 157
Ming, W. R., Jr., 22, 48, 49, 89, 122, 147
Minnesota, 144, 145, 151
Minsky, Joseph, 123
Mississippi, 123
Missouri, 110, 134, 143, 147
Moody, Blair, 144
Moos, Malcolm, 150
Mowrer, Edgar Ansel, 14

Murrow, Edward R., 170
Muskie, E. S., 110
Myers, Francis J., 77, 88, 89, 100, 101, 102, 103, 110, 111–14, 121, 122, 128, 129, 130, 133, 140, 145, 163

Nangle, John, 110
Nashville Tennessean, 115
National Committee Stevenson for President, 28, 52, 56, 83, 114, 163, 164; *see also* Draft Stevenson Committee
National Guard Armory, 3, 5
New Jersey, 72, 77, 80, 86, 100, 110, 121, 123, 132, 134, 163, 167
Newman, Ralph, 68
New Republic, 24
Newsweek, 28, 37, 45, 113, 169
New York City, 29, 31, 118
New York Daily News, 67, 115
New York Herald Tribune, 23, 24, 115
New York Journal-American, 115
New York Post, 29, 32, 112, 115, 117, 130
New York State, 110
New York Times, 27, 28, 29, 30, 33, 49, 61, 65–6, 68, 72, 80, 104, 115, 133, 142, 143, 147, 159, 160
North Carolina, 76, 84, 110
Northwestern University, 13
Norton, Howard, 63, 65, 113

Official Report of the Proceedings of the Democratic National Convention, 149
Ohio, 69–70, 76, 80, 81, 110, 121
Oregon, 27, 35, 110
Overton, George, 21, 34, 47, 118

Palmer, Dwight, 77, 110
Pastore, John O., 110
Patterson, La Fayette, 110
Patterson, Okey L., 111
Pennsylvania, 77, 80, 86, 88, 90, 92, 95–6, 98, 100, 101–3, 110, 114, 120, 122, 123, 132, 145, 151, 163, 167
Perlman, Philip B., 75
Petersky, Sanford, 84, 110–11
Petrie, Donald, 21
Philadelphia, 29, 77, 86, 96, 136
Philadelphia Bulletin, 89
Philadelphia Democratic Committee, 98
Phinizy, Coles H., 62
Pickens, Anna G., 123
Pickett, T. J., 71
Pierce, Franklin, 71
Pike, Otis G., 110
Pittsburgh, 29, 81, 98, 101
Polk, James K., 71
Pope, Alexander, 48
Portland, Me., 27
Portland, Me., *Press-Herald,* 27
Portland, Ore., 35
Presidential Nominating Politics in 1952 (David, Moos, and Goldman), 150, 167
Princeton University, 12, 86
Pusey, Merlo J., 83

Raleigh News and Observer, 75–6
Rayburn, Sam, 149
Reporter, 33, 132, 146, 150
Republican Convention, 1952, 36, 42, 45, 75
Republican Party, 96, 106, 108, 143, 145, 160, 168
Reston, James, 49, 65–6, 104, 132
Reuther, Walter, 85, 124
Rhode Island, 110
Riggs, Robert L., 49, 61

Ringler, Paul, 44, 100
Roberts, Dorothy, 123
Roberts, Willa Mae, 110
Robichaud, Gerry, 61
Roosevelt, Eleanor, 14, 34
Roosevelt, Franklin Delano, 75, 106
Roosevelt, Franklin Delano, Jr., 144, 145, 147
Roosevelt, James, 136
Rose, Alex, 169
Rosenbloom, Irving J., 21, 48, 147
Rosenfield, Maurice, 22, 48, 132
Russell, Richard, 20, 28, 45, 59, 76, 125, 141, 149, 150, 151, 153

Sachs, Bernard, 48
St. Louis Post-Dispatch, 24, 28, 63, 66, 116, 157
San Francisco, 14
San Francisco Chronicle, 115
San Francisco Examiner, 115
Sasscer, L. G., 135
Saturday Evening Post, 28
Schricker, Henry F., 36, 64–8, 72, 81, 101, 102–3, 110, 111, 113, 128, 131, 132, 137–40, 141, 142
Seattle, 29
Seattle Times, 29
Sevareid, Eric, 125–6, 170
Sevareid, Peter, 170
Sharlette, Jesse R., 110
Sherman, John, 70
Sherman, William Tecumseh, 25, 26, 79, 116, 156
Shocknessy, James, 110
Shriver, R. Sargent, Jr., 117
Simpson, Barbara, 48
Smith, H. Alexander, 80
Smith, Theodore C., 69
Solon, Joseph, 22, 49, 139
South Carolina, 145, 146

Soviet Union, 107
Springfield (Ill.), 26, 27, 56, 72
State Journal (Lincoln, Neb.), 160
Stettinius, Edward R., Jr., 14
Stevens, Lewis M., 86, 87, 89
Stevenson, Adlai (grandfather), 7, 15, 63
Stevenson, Borden, 57–9
Stevenson, John Fell, 57–9
Stevenson, Lewis Green, 7, 15, 63
Stevenson and the Independent Voter (De Voto), 24
Stevenson for Governor Committee, 25
Stokes, Thomas L., 67, 78
Stone, Victor, 123
Sweetland, Monroe, 110

Tacoma, 29
Taft, Robert A., 71, 75, 116
Taylor, Zachary, 71
Teefy, William, 89, 98, 121
Texas, 35
That Reminds Me (Barkley), 124
Tillett, Mrs. Charles, 76
Time, 15, 16, 18, 164
Truman, Harry S., 4–5, 14, 18–19, 27, 31, 37, 60, 75, 80, 85, 108, 128, 134, 135, 143, 150, 152, 153–4, 159, 166, 169

United Hatters, Cap and Millinery Workers Union, 169
United Nations, 14, 106
United Press, 50
U.S. News & World Report, 28
United States Senate, 50, 64, 84, 162
University of Chicago, 48, 132, 164
University of Chicago Round Table, 48

Utah, 121
Utley, Clifton, 78

Van Buren, Martin, 71
Vandenberg, Arthur, 14
Vermont, 70
Virginia, 145, 146, 147
Vosse, Fred, 123

Wallace, Mike, 148
Wall Street Journal, 53
Warren, Earl, 45
Washington, 110, 111
Washington, D.C., 3, 4, 13, 17, 48, 50, 84, 86
Washington Post, 63, 115, 163
Washington Star, 45, 63, 103, 115
Watertown, N.Y., *Times*, 45
Watson, George, 123

Webster, Daniel, 71
West Virginia, 111
Whatley, Barney L., 110
White, William Allen, 13
White, William S., 143
Whitecotton, Howard, 101
White House, 4, 19, 71, 75, 158
Will, Hubert, 21, 48, 49, 76, 79, 89, 101, 102, 122, 149
Williams, G. Mennen, 68, 141, 144, 151
Willkie, Wendell, 116
Wilson, James, 111
Wilson, Woodrow, 11, 108, 153, 160
Wiseman, Al, 48

Yates, Sidney, 22, 48, 101, 110
Yellon, Donald, 123
Young, John, 77, 110

A NOTE ON THE TYPE

This book is set in Electra, a Linotype face designed by W. A. Dwiggins. This face cannot be classified as either modern or old-style. It is not based on any historical model, nor does it echo any particular period or style. It avoids the extreme contrast between thick and thin elements that marks most modern faces, and attempts to give a feeling of fluidity, power, and speed.

Typographic and binding designs are by W. A. Dwiggins.

The book was composed, printed, and bound by Kingsport Press, Inc., Kingsport, Tennessee.

Typography based on designs by W. A. Dwiggins.